NAVIGATING CHANGE

(My Story)

Timeless Secrets for Growth in an Ever-Changing World

Niyi Borire

© 2020 Niyi Borire

All rights reserved. No portion of this book may be reproduced, stored in a retrieval system, or transmitted in any form or by any means – electronic, mechanical, photocopy, recording, scanning, or others except for brief quotations in critical reviews or articles, without the prior written permission of the author and publisher.

Contact

Website: niyiborire.com

Facebook: Niyi Borire

Instagram: @niyi_borire

DEDICATION

This book is dedicated to the two most important women in my life – my wife and my mum.

My mum birthed me, watched my first steps, and saw my first smile

To my wife, Olayemi, the woman who keeps me grounded and has got my back. The woman who adores me so much yet is bold enough to preach my sermons back to me.

ACKNOWLEDGEMENTS

This book would not have been possible without the foundational support I have received from my parents over the years. Special thanks to my late dad, Andrew DaRocha Borire, who provided me with a sure academic foundation that created a thirst for knowledge and excellence in me. To my mum, who is always there for me, praying for me, encouraging me, and is one of my greatest fans – I owe her a lot of appreciation.

I also want to thank my siblings, Funke, Lara, Gbenga, and Gbemisola, without whom my story would not be complete. My sincere appreciation to all those who laboured on the manuscript, including Eno, Jennifer, and Jack.

My gratitude is also extended to my friends; Tofunmi, Samuel (The Purpose Preacher), Herve, Dunni, Senayon, Paul, and Omor.

I could not have achieved anything without the support of my wife, Olayemi. I owe her my deepest gratitude for her unwavering support throughout the process of writing this book. I would also like to thank our two sons, Daniel and Ethan. You mean the world to me, and my message of change is meaningless without you in my life.

CONTENTS

Navigating Change (My Story)

DEDICATION 3

CONTENTS 4

FOREWORD 6

PROLOGUE 9

A POSITIVE APPROACH 11

DISCOVERING PURPOSE 23

DREAMER BOY 43

RELATIONSHIPS 58

INTEGRITY 81

EXPLOITS OF FAITH 90

PERSISTENCE 103

EPILOGUE 116

CONCLUSION 119

COMMENTARY 123

FOREWORD

Change, it has been said, is a permanent feature of human society, history, and human nature. Change is good evidence of life. We live in a time of change when things are happening so fast that it's breathtaking to catch up with them. Where there are growth and development, change is to be expected. Our lives will keep changing, our environment will keep changing, people around us will keep changing, our situation and circumstance will keep changing. Fashion has changed; shapes and designs of our buildings are changing; our knowledge of the world around us has changed. People's interests, priorities, family life, jobs, friends, and values have changed. Change is inevitable in the final analysis.

While certain changes will happen TO US, affecting our personal lives, families, and careers, other changes happen AROUND US, affecting our society, nation, or world and which will impact us personally. Furthermore, while certain changes will happen WITH US that will affect who we are, either physically, emotionally, mentally, or spiritually, other changes will happen FOR US and AMONG US in order to take advantage of certain opportunities.

When it comes to change, we must learn not to ignore or deny or be angry at it. We must also learn not to resist or defy it or accept it in a fatalistic way. We should not just watch change happen; nor should we just talk about or question it, but learn how to get better – not bitter – with what's thrown at us.

Anyone who wants to work and walk with God to navigate through a time of change must realise that He is a God of principles. As far as He is concerned, there are certain rules or laws which if engaged will ensure preservation, protection, maintenance, maximum performance, proper functioning, and fulfillment of purpose. God's principles – various aspects of which the author has used – are permanent, unchangeable, immutable, and constant. His principles can be universally applied with equal success. Divine principles where employed, although they may seem to limit our choices, are known to protect us and ours against damage, harm, and destruction. Divine principles, when understood and obeyed, assure that everything will turn out as planned by God.

What this book has done is to open our eyes to the fact that although we may not be able to plan and prepare for all changes, as some are unexpected, we can oversee and manage change even when it involves painful groanings. It is such proper handling and control that we can bring to bear using some principles that are highlighted in Niyi's book. This will help us integrate well with the change occurring and that will make us grow and even thrive as we navigate some challenging seasons of our lives. God's Word contains the principles that are expected to govern our lives if we are going to fulfil His purpose for us. And the more we bring our lives in line with the Word, the more we will operate by His divine principles and thus better our lives.

The author of this book has given us in a very simple, casually readable form – using a whole lot of his personal experiences through life – biblical, time tested, and working principles that illustrate richly and generously that we can navigate through changes successfully. Indeed, let it be known that with total dependence on the Holy Spirit, you can discover your purpose in life, be driven forward by a new way of thinking, learn new truths, and exhibit a dogged determination to never quit while remaining positive. Learning that by having enriching vital relationships with others (whom we should listen to), we can make wise choices and decisions.

You have made a correct choice by getting this book, so read it and implement its every message for your growth – even as you groan.

REV. GEORGE ADEGBOYE

President, Rhema Chapel International Churches

London, UK.

6th October 2020.

Navigating Change (My Story)

PROLOGUE

Change is derived from an old Latin word, *Cambire,* which literally means barter or trade. So, change is a trade-off between the present and the future. It is unavoidable in our lives. Change is a constant force of life that cannot be resisted by our present situation, circumstances, or achievements. But change can also be painful and difficult to endure because we are accustomed to a certain way of life. Our cultures, customs, and our traditions have been deeply encoded into our minds. This deep hard-wired connection between our experiences and our minds makes it difficult for us to adapt to change or respond to change positively.

John Maxwell said, *"Change is inevitable, but growth is optional."*

Understanding the inevitability and unavoidability of change is important, but our *response* to change is much more important. Our response to our changing world and changing environment will go a long way in determining what we get out of life. So many people struggle to make the necessary adjustments when they are faced with change; either sudden and unexpected or slow and progressive change.

I have had my fair share of change, just like everyone else. I have suffered the trauma of being sexually abused as a child. I've had to leave an expensive private school to go to an under-funded, public community school because my dad's business collapsed. I have been through a situation where I was thrust into being the breadwinner of the family, following the sudden demise of my father. I've chosen to take the bold step of leaving my country of birth to pursue my dreams in a new country. However, having gone through all these different changes in my life, I realised that what has kept me going and helped me to achieve this level of success is my response to all these changing situations.

Irrespective of the tempo and extent of change, our preparedness and approach will determine whether we will grow from it, or we will groan through it. Growth is optional, and it seems it is not for everyone. Change in itself is difficult, but to grow in a changing situation is extremely painful for the self. How so? If you are going to grow up, you've got to *give up* something. Growth involves sacrifice. Growth involves letting go. Growth involves stretching beyond one's limits. That is only possible when we are ready to face our changing world positively.

In this book, I describe the seven secrets I have learnt from my own life that helped me navigate the changing circumstances I have gone through. I hope that by reading this book and applying the principles into your life, you will be able to go through a similar journey of growth to mine, as I adapted to and faced change.

Let's survive change.

Navigating Change (My Story)

Chapter 1

A Positive Approach

On a sunny Sunday morning, I strode purposefully into the male medical ward – a ward that admits many but discharges a few – hoping to just say hello to dear old dad and zoom off to church. On entering the ward, I was greeted by the matron's voice, '*Doctor Borire, we lost your daddy*'. It was like a dream. A jolt sent shivers down my spine, like a patient under a defibrillator. I went over to his bed, lifted the white blanket, and stared at his breathless body. On his face was a restful smile. '*O death, where is thy sting? O grave, where is thy victory*'?

A sojourn of over sixty years had just come to an end. Twice he had cheated death, but not this time. Standing there, regret hung its heavy burden on my shoulders. This was my lowest point in life and it was so devastating. Even so, I've learnt that there is always a gift in every pain. Your greatness lies in your capacity to handle this pain. At this level of pain, many people miss it. They end up committing suicide or falling sick out of depression. Life can be so unfair at times. It's full of ups and downs. Just as the electrocardiogram of someone who is still alive is never a straight line. As long as your heart pumps, it goes up and down. I had my share of pain and grief. I understand perfectly what it feels like to get knocked down by the storms of life. Yet, I took my pain and squeezed out the gift inside it. If I could sail through, you can. Perhaps, you should read my story.

In 2008, my father told me he had a wound on his leg that was not healing, yet each time I suggested visiting the hospital, he would decline. As weeks went by, the wound got worse. As a medical student, I knew that this was not a condition to ignore, so I insisted. After so much persuasion, he finally agreed and I took him to the hospital for a checkup. The doctors confirmed our worst fears; the circulation in his legs had been compromised, presumably by diabetes. His blood sugar was so high that it was unrecordable on a glucometer. He had little or no blood flow in his foot, and this had stopped the wound from healing.

Apparently, the wound had become infected and the infection was already spreading to other parts of his body. We were advised to have his leg amputated. I watched the look on my dad's face and I could tell he was in pain. He refused to accept the doctor's advice at first but the medics prevailed and reluctantly he went for surgery. After the amputation, things got complicated because of the poor medical system in Nigeria. Daily, the infection got worse. He suffered from bedsores and was bedridden. It was horrible seeing him lose weight. He had come in with an infected wound on his foot and ended up having a below-knee amputation with multiple revisions. The family racked up thousands of dollars for his treatments over three months, which culminated in huge unpaid bills. All my life savings had gone into this and, as life would have it, this was the same period I was planning to travel for my Australian exams. Getting his body out of the mortuary was so difficult due to our financial crisis. As honest citizens, it was an embarrassment for our family. And we were all confused about where to turn for

Navigating Change (My Story)

assistance. It seemed the whole world was crumbling on us. Soon, I summoned enough courage to approach one of the hospital's directors, who was also deputised as a Professor of Pathology.

Knowing the stakes, I confidently introduced myself to him as one of his former students and quickly reminded him of the distinction I had in his course. He was kind enough to facilitate the release of my father's body without any payment. The hospital board also erased our debt and released his death certificate without any fuss. What a great relief! Dad was buried in his hometown in Southwest Nigeria. One day in November 2008 is a moment I can never forget. The family stood united at the open-air funeral, each with gloomy faces, as we gave dad our last respects. I looked at his corpse and I had to accept this fate. The image is forever entrenched in my soul. We lowered him into the grave as we performed the last rites. After the funeral, harsh reality stared me in the face. Without a penny in my pocket, I took out a loan to pay for my exams in Australia. I could have sat down at home to weep, but instead, I took up the challenge to move on after the medical system had failed me. As the first son, I was certain that if I didn't do something quickly, my entire family would remain in abject poverty. I hated 'our' poverty. I hated the fact that we were practically living from hand to mouth; this motivated me. Sometimes, pain can be a man's greatest drive. Amid this pain, I embraced positivity as I realised that several responsibilities rested on my shoulders. It was up to me. I spent cold nights studying hard for my Australian exams. For me, this was my last resort. Every night I drifted off with thoughts about my father's demise and how life would still go on.

My father and I didn't have a close relationship until the end of his life. The first time he ever told me he loved me was on his dying bed and this touched me deeply. Growing up with him, I had never seen this side of my father. He held me with his frail arms and appreciated me for looking after him. His words melted my heart. Goosebumps spread over my skin as I looked into his jaundiced eyes dumbfounded. Irrespective of how low our relationship was, I let the past remain in the past and hugged him close. So when he died, I missed him. I was determined to look after the rest of the family and I was ready to do everything legitimately possible to fight the poverty that had crippled us at the time. I studied harder.

***

Australia first came to my attention in 2008 via a BBC documentary about Australia's need for international doctors. It was a PR move sponsored by the Howard government, aimed at attracting overseas trained doctors to fill in specialist positions in Australia. They portrayed doctors from all over the world, including the United Kingdom, India, Russia, and the Philippines, who had successfully migrated and been integrated into the Australian health system. It all seemed to make sense and I felt like I had just had my Eureka moment. Getting the study materials for an Australian exam was another challenge in my path. I had shared my dream of travelling to Australia with five of my fellow interns and they were really excited about taking this leap with me. We all contributed money to buy one of the recommended textbooks because that was all we could afford. Life was that hard. I surfed the Internet for online materials and did thorough research. Obviously, I had switched focus from the trauma at home to the glint of a good future ahead of me. The past was already gone and there was nothing I could have done to bring my father back to life. I had watched on helplessly as the under-funded medical system and ineffective drugs snatched life out of him. I just wanted to move to another country and experience a new environment and practice. Even though it was a difficult decision to make, I was convinced to pursue my dreams at all costs.

I applied for a tourist visa to Australia and fortunately, my application was approved. During this period, I still had no hope of buying my flight tickets out of Nigeria. I made a list of people I would ask for assistance, but they all turned me down. At this point, I was at a crossroads, thinking of my forthcoming exams. Cancelling the trip meant that the exam fee I had struggled to pay would go down the drain with nothing to show for it. Such a dilemma! I couldn't imagine missing the only opportunity I had to pursue my dream career.

It was January 2009 and my phone beeped. It was a call from my mentor, Mr. Ayo Awe. This was unbelievable because I wasn't expecting his call and it came just in the nick of time. Mr. Awe apologised for not keeping in touch with me. He knew about my travel plans to Australia because I had watched that BBC documentary on doctor opportunities while in his house. He asked about my travelling to Australia and I told him it was on hold due to the lack of funds. I could not finance my trip after my father's healthcare and funeral expenses. Mr. Awe promised to support me. Three days later, I received a whopping sum of money, enough to pay for my flight ticket. I was super excited as I hurried to the travel agency to book my flight. That was the single biggest gift I had ever received in my entire life.

On my way to the airport, I saw my good friend, Kunle, whom I convinced to accompany me to the airport. I had earlier emptied my account which luckily contained the exact amount needed to buy the cheapest South African Airways flight ticket to

Australia, according to the online source. However, when I got to the counter, I was told the price of the ticket had gone up. I needed more money to book my flight, running into hundreds of dollars. I was gobsmacked since I had only checked the price online less than an hour prior and it was hard to believe that the price rose in less than one hour. It was barely two weeks to my Australian exam and I was determined to get my ticket that day. Going home and returning the next day was not an option either, because I knew the price would rise further. Kunle and I stood there gazing at each other, not knowing what to do. We pleaded for a discount, all to no avail. It was at that point Kunle remembered that he had just collected some money from his brother that day – the exact amount I needed to complete the payment. What a miracle! Kunle was very nice; he gave me the money and I booked my flight that day. I jumped for joy. The first phase was solved but the second phase wasn't. I wondered what it would be like travelling to Australia with absolutely no money to lodge in a hotel or eat. Getting accommodation was my next big problem. Being bankrupt, I had no means to support myself for more than a week in Australia. Then came some good news. One of my former classmates had a brother in Western Australia who offered to accommodate me for a few months. I thought that this was the answer to my prayers but I was wrong. His house was in Morawa, a rural town, while my exam was to take place in Perth, more than 400 kilometres away! I still needed to find a roof over my head in Perth.

While sitting in the doctors' lounge in Lagos, I had overheard one of my colleagues talking about a senior colleague who lived in Perth. Quickly, I logged into Facebook, which was a relatively new social media platform at that time, and searched for her name, Dr. Martins. Thankfully, I found her profile, sent her a friend request, and got her phone number. We started chatting

Navigating Change (My Story)

and I finally told her about my trip to Perth for the medical exam. She congratulated me and I got to know that our parents attended the same church. What a divine arrangement! Somehow, I had never met her before. After I told her that I had nowhere to stay in Perth, she asked me to hang on while she talked to her husband about it. She was willing to support me and she accommodated me all through the exam week in Perth. Studying was still difficult for me when reading through past questions because a glance at every page reminded me of the death of my father in Nigeria. Studying in that condition was stressful; notwithstanding, I had to. From Perth, I moved to Morawa, a very small town. I lived with a Nigerian family, the Bolarinwas, while I searched for jobs, but my efforts were in vain. All the job agencies I contacted rejected me. They saw me as a new graduate from Nigeria with little medical experience, someone who had nothing to offer. My visa was about to expire and I was still stuck in a new country, searching for a job. I didn't have work experience that matched the Australian medical standards at that time, so I got knocked back over and over again. This was a difficult time for me. The financial pressure was so much that I wondered how I would ever repay the money I had borrowed to travel. I had spent the $500 I travelled with and had no money elsewhere. I was dependent on the Bolarinwas for my necessities. Facing this struggle daily, I was at my lowest point. I kept applying for jobs, but being rejected was the order of the day for me. According to the agents, I wasn't qualified since I was only an intern.

One day, an agent advised me to go back to Nigeria for my good because Australian hospitals pay them large sums of money to provide experienced doctors, not newbies. This first-world country did not want people who would be trained; they wanted people who were already trained and experienced. About this time, I stumbled on the contact details of John Hamilton, a Professor of Medicine at the University of Newcastle. He had visited my medical school a year before to give a lecture. That was where I got the opportunity of meeting him. He had assured me that Australia was a wonderful place to pursue physician training. Unfortunately, he did not respond to any of my emails. I resorted to lowering my standards and quitting the search for medical officer positions. I began to apply for health support positions, such as health care assistant and disability support worker, or any other job that could earn me income. Time was ticking; I was on a tourist visa with less than two months left before it expired. I needed an employer to sponsor me, so I could get my work permit, but this was not happening. Finally, my exam results were out and I had passed, but alas I still couldn't get a job. For the few menial jobs available, only citizens and permanent residents were eligible for these low paying positions. No organisation would sponsor a work permit for someone to clean the toilet! Things got worse when I had overstayed my welcome with the Bolarinwas. We had only agreed that I would be there for about a month or two, but I was stuck staying in their home because I had no job or income. I was not contributing to the house management, so they had the right to ask me to leave. This torture broke my heart deeply.

The situation was unbearable and winter only made it worse. Coming from the warm climate of Nigeria to a much colder environment was challenging and it was another big ordeal for me. I cried most nights, soaking my pillow with tears. I was afraid that I would never make any progress. My visa was almost expiring and this reminded me of the sad reality that I would go back to Nigeria with nothing to fall back on. This constant miserable feeling made me depressed and I withdrew from social interactions. However, even amid this sadness, there was

Navigating Change (My Story)

still a little hope in my heart. I didn't understand it at first, but I soon discovered that every battle I had overcome in the past gave me a new morsel of confidence for bigger battles.

Sometimes, when you are in the deepest hole and you remember how you got out of previous painful holes miraculously, you get an assurance that you can come out of your current predicament. Since the Australian agents had written me off, I began to think of a plan B. One day, I walked up to the council offices of Morawa shire, a town of 600 people and about 400 kilometres north of Perth. The Chief Executive Officer's name was Gavin Treasure. When I approached Gavin, I was at my lowest and felt I had nothing to lose. The worst I would hear was a NO! I introduced myself as a doctor and he seemed glad to see me. Surprisingly, he patiently listened to me and was quite moved by my story. Apparently, the shire had been searching for a doctor to back-up the resident GP who had been in the area for a few years and was planning to move to Geraldton, a much bigger city. Gavin saw my potential and was willing to offer me a contract to work in the local clinic. However, there was a big impediment – the Medical Board.

The Board would not register me as an independent medical practitioner due to my lack of experience. So, I decided to get creative. I went back home and created a new role with a distinct job description that had not previously existed: Assistant GP (Medical Officer in General Practice). This role would allow me to work under the supervision of the local GP who also backed the idea and was willing to supervise me. I made sure the job description favoured my Curriculum Vitae (CV). I also put together the eligibility criteria and reporting structure.

The next day, I took it to Gavin and he was quite impressed. He got the shire to adopt the proposal and the new role was immediately advertised. He offered me the contract and we applied to the Western Australian Medical Board. We also applied to the immigration department for a work permit. At this time, my tourist visa was one week from expiration. Luckily, I was offered a bridging visa by the immigration department while my application for a medical licence was being processed. The bridging visa allowed me to stay in the country but, I still couldn't work until I got a licence from the Medical Board. I had been scheduled for an interview by the board, before the approval of my licence. While I was waiting for my licence, Professor John Hamilton finally replied. I was on a bridging visa at that time. If I had not taken the initiative to approach the shire council with a creative idea, John's reply would have gotten to me when back in Nigeria – far too late for me. He was impressed by my courage to pursue a career in Australia against all odds, especially because I just lost my father. After another email, he linked me up with the medical superintendent at John Hunter Hospital Newcastle, and I was offered a position as a medical doctor. This was a dream come true for me.

Now, I was given two job opportunities at the same time. Of course, my initial quest was to become a neurologist, so I accepted this job. I reported back to Gavin with fear that he would be upset that I put him through so much stress, but instead he was happy for me. In fact, he congratulated me and asked me to go ahead. This was how I moved from an insignificant Nigerian intern to an employed doctor in the Australian health system.

***

Navigating Change (My Story)

Each time I reflect on the struggles I've been through, I get inspired to reach out to humanity. If I was not determined to succeed, I would have spent the rest of my life thinking *I am not good enough*. Just like the heartbeat line of life, success is not a straight road. Tough times will arise, but it is up to you to rewrite your story. A positive approach to life will eradicate regret from your life. It's often said that life is 1% what happens to you and 99% how you react to it. When you try to be as optimistic as possible despite the challenges, you will begin to see yourself rise. Despite my pain through those years, I kept the hope alive. The future you desire is in your hands to create. What are you creating? Your attitude towards life, positive or negative, makes the difference. It doesn't matter how heavy the storms are, what matters is how determined you are to create your own sunshine. There are no limitations to your success, except for the one you have created for yourself. The only thing that exists is a stumbling block, which of course is what life throws at everyone. Your responsibility is to jump over each one and climb the heights to the other side where your greatness lies. Let me share with you a few ways you can achieve that:

Fill Your Mind with Positivity

Beginning your day with positivity is the highest form of living a great life. Read books with positive messages. Listen to music with uplifting lyrics. Listen to inspiring podcast episodes. Surround yourself with positive-thinking individuals. Change your attitude for the better by filling up your mind with the needed nutrients for boosting your morale. Focus on the good in your life and the good in others. Instead of waiting for external things to make you happy, just be happy and then watch how that influences the things around you. Happiness is an attitude, not a situation.

Watch Your Language

If you want to grow as a person, you might need to change your language if it is full of negativity. Statements such as, *"I can't do that"* only encourage you to think that way. If you say something is impossible, you'll likely believe it. So, use positive language such as, *"I can do this if I take it step by step"* or *"I will get this breakthrough"* or *"I see myself succeeding in this"*. Once you get used to having positive conversations with your inner self and making good affirmations, you will experience a change of perception. While it is good to have a positive mindset, take a few minutes to imagine the end goal. Think about the obstacles in your way and balance the fantasy.

Be Grateful for Little Wins

Also, take time to think about what you are thankful for. Embrace the powerful virtue called gratitude. Maybe you can come up with three things each day that you appreciate and write them in a journal. This shows you in clear terms that you are winning, little by little. Even though I had no job in Australia, the fact that I left Nigeria successfully and passed my Australian examination was a little win which I was grateful for. That motivated me to keep pushing until I won. Remember, there will always be light at the end of a long dark tunnel, so reach for it.

Chapter 2

Discovering Purpose

Purpose is the most important force ever in the life of a person. A lot of people have talked about purpose, what purpose is, and why it is important. You can only understand why discovering my purpose was important to me if you understand my background. For me, understanding my purpose gave my life meaning. It gave me a sense of direction. It made me more effective in my life. There is no way that I could have achieved all that I have achieved today if I did not strive to discover my purpose. In my early twenties, I remember hearing somebody talk powerfully about purpose. I was drawn to this. I wanted to understand what my purpose was. That was because I was in a difficult situation and my quality of life was not up to the standard that I would have liked. Amid the poverty, I was trying to find a sense of meaning. That spurred me on to pursue my purpose. I was in a practically dysfunctional family. My parents were at odds with each other and they fought often. As far as I was concerned, they had a failed marriage. All of this stemmed from the fact that my father, who was doing very well for a good while, had a problem with his business. In fact, his business collapsed. My father was a Printer. He had a printing business and printed at an industrial scale – books, materials for governments and banks, etc. In the late 70s and early 80s, most of the stationery and processes of different companies and banks were paper-based, so there was a lot of printing to do. We were, therefore, quite comfortable. I remember that when my dad started his business in the 80s, he was doing quite well. He would tell me stories of him taking my mom on a weekend date from Lagos to London. He would pick her up on a Friday night from work. She worked in NITEL (the National telecommunications company) as a supervisor. On a Friday night, he would whisk her off to London (on fairly cheap tickets). They would go on a Friday evening and return to Lagos by Sunday evening, all without a visa. Just a six-hour flight to London, where they would have fun. Sometimes, they would go from London on a train to Paris or Amsterdam, then back to London before flying back to Lagos. It wasn't a big deal. They were middle class, but they were comfortable. My mum was exposed to different cultures and had been to half of Europe by the time she was in her mid-twenties. She had friends all over – from Luxemburg, to Paris, to Belgium. Despite this fun, my parents struggled in their marriage. For a while, my dad had a good business while my mum stayed at home after she was made redundant. There was no more need for her to work because they were comfortable at that point. But things changed when my father's business collapsed. He got a contract that failed, which led to the demise of his business. Once the business collapsed and there was no more money coming through, they started quarrelling and fighting a lot. While this book is not about their story, it is important to understand the context: I was a young kid who saw how my parents related with each other very poorly. Mum often accused dad of cheating or of not playing his breadwinning role. He would then hit back, '*But what are you*

Navigating Change (My Story)

doing?' He felt wronged under this pressure. The trouble always ended with my father physically abusing my mum. It was pretty violent at times. At times, my mum was humiliated. I can't forget those nights when I saw my dad abuse my mom. It scarred my mind. As a small child hiding under the covers, it was frightening. It was not long before my older sister and I were invited to a birthday party, but my father did not want us to go. My mum didn't understand why because the friends were very close to us. In fact, the party girl was my classmate and her mum was my mum's close friend. Still, my dad insisted that we couldn't go. When the argument progressed, it became physical and my father beat the hell out of my mum. He locked us in the room and really trashed her over a silly argument about attending a child's birthday party. Neighbours came in as usual; they were not blind or deaf to it. Although we ended up going, it was messed up. I was probably only 5 or 6, but I can't forget. I can't forget where my mother was, where my father was, where I was, how we were crying and screaming. Things did not get better. After a while, there was a lot of distrust and my father wanted to leave. He was certainly not happy in the marriage. My mum was not happy either. They couldn't work it out. They were not people of faith, although they were churchgoers. In fact, my father was an elder in the church, but he was not a born again Christian and he knew it. Even though he was an elder in the church, he was still doing a lot of things that he knew were wrong. They were merely churchgoers, so there was no way they could help each other by using the principles of the Bible. They were just tearing each other apart. My prayer as a kid was, '*God, I don't want to have this type of marriage.*' They were two strong personalities, neither willing to back down for the other, and it was explosive. It affected all of us. I was psychologically scarred, to the point where I just did not want to have anything to do with being at home. It has affected me, until now, to the extent that I do not have a close relationship with my family. It drove me away from home at the tender age of 14. Since then, I have never really been back home. That was how toxic it was. The home was chaotic for me. Finances were bad. After the business loss, my dad had nothing else going for him. My mum had been a stay-at-home mom for over a decade. They were both used to a high-class lifestyle – travelling, enjoying, partying – but all of that disappeared and it was chaotic. I can't forget those days when we had nothing. I remember that my mum would give away her clothes just to get us food. It was that bad. I remember a Christmas day where we had nothing, absolutely nothing to eat. All we had was unripe plantain and palm oil. We boiled the unripe plantain and it was horrible. It tasted like glue. We had to dip it in palm oil. No sauce, nothing. It was terrible. And that was Christmas morning for us. In the evening, we had to just pray that our neighbours would bring food. Thank God they did, because that was how we ate. Life was difficult. I remember there was a day, while my father was still around, we had no money in the house. My dad, mum, and five children searched everywhere but we found no money. It was ridiculous to me. I remember a day I took textbooks to a woman on the street who hawked bean cake. We exchanged the meal for the books. It was that bad. On top of all of that, we were drifting apart. The whole family was always arguing and fighting each other. There was a day I got so angry that I threw my hot plate of food on my sister's face. We would tear each other apart. None of us was happy. The atmosphere wasn't good at all. In all of this, I would cry and say, *'God, why am I here'*? I remember I would peep through the neighbour's windows to watch the 1996 Olympic Games then. We had no working television. We had no car. I always questioned myself, *'God, why? Why was I born into this home? Why am I unhappy? Why do we lack basic supplies? Why do we have nothing'*? And when I heard any loud thud at home, my heart started racing. I'd instinctively think there was another fight. That too made me sad. When I was in junior secondary school, I did not have a school bag. My school bag was a sack, like a Coles shopping bag. I didn't have shoes. I used my older sister's shoes for over two years. Oh, the embarrassment of wearing female sandals to school and worn-out clothes. My school uniform was torn. I would walk to school with my 'bag' in my arms. Going to school was tough. I questioned everything – my future, my life, why I was born into the family I was born into. I just was not a happy person.

Picture: *My graduation from primary school (St Bernadette's Primary School, Lagos) in 1991*

I was in a private and prestigious secondary school when my father's business collapsed, but without money for fees, I had to be withdrawn and started to attend a public school. The public school was in a sorry state. It was heavily underfunded, with a few teachers and poor amenities. There was a time our class did not have a chemistry teacher, so we had to learn chemistry by ourselves. Thankfully, I got a distinction, though as I said, it was tough. On top of that, I started moving with the wrong crowd. I became a troublemaker because I was angry. I joined this gang in school that would stay behind after class to foment trouble. I was one of the smallest in class, but I walked with the big boys, so I was protected. I delivered the love letters for the big boys. I ran errands for them, but I got protection so nobody could touch me. They taught me how to approach girls and gave me different lines to use, e.g. *'I'll like to be your bee, you be my gee'*. But I never had the boldness to approach any girl because I was so small. However, I was well coached! In return, I taught them physics since I was one of the most brilliant students in the class. School, for me, was a means of release. I loved school because I didn't want to be at home. At home, there was too much conflict, we had little money, and oftentimes no electricity. But in school, I just had fun. In summary, this provides a background of my difficult personal circumstances. There was only one compensation, which was that I was academically gifted. I never failed an exam.

How did I Discover My Purpose?

Two key principles that made a difference for me were:

1. Understanding the internal processes of my mind and my values.
2. My external experiences.

To discover your purpose, you must rely on those internal processes, your values, and external experiences that resonate.

Navigating Change (My Story)

The key to knowing my true purpose was my core values. I realised that even though I struggled with many challenges and was raised in a difficult situation, at the core, I had empathy. At my very core, I had a deep care for vulnerable people. This was obviously drawn out from my experience of going through tough times. I still get very emotional when I see people going through times of hardship. It touches me deeply. When I see others going through tough times, I find myself willing to go the extra mile to do what I have to do. So, I began to notice that my purpose was to help vulnerable people. I was really a 'people person'. Most of that stemmed from my character. And I realised that if I was going to be fulfilled in life, I would have to find myself a place or position where I could respond to the needs of vulnerable people, lift them from whatever situation they were in, and help them to fulfil their potential. That was my purpose. So, whatever I could do to reach out to people who were sick, vulnerable, poor, despondent, or going through tough times, I would do it. Whether I would achieve that through my faith, my career, or through my family, that was it.

Lesson: Look at your core values and inner character to discover your purpose.

The second indicator for me was my gifts. This academic prowess was the biggest compensation that I had. Even though things were tough at home, I was academically sound. While in primary school, a teacher observed my aptitude and so I skipped a class twice. While everyone else went through year one, I went straight from kindergarten to year two. When I got to class on my first day of year two, the teacher was writing a sentence on the board that was quite long and could not fit onto a single line. This was different from the short one-liner sentences I was used to in kindergarten. Coming to year two and seeing the teacher write a long sentence was confounding. We were asked to copy the sentence, but I could not. I scribbled, but it wouldn't fit into one line. I repeatedly erased it and tried to squeeze everything into one line. I did not understand that I could go to the next line and continue the sentence. I tried it over and over again until I started crying. The teacher came over to ask what was wrong. '*It won't fit*', I wept. He said, '*No, you can just continue on the next line*'. My four-year-old self said, '*Okay*' and continued. Out of the 23 students in the class, my position after the first term was number 23. After the second term, I was in the fifth position. After term three, I was in the first position in the class. My parents were right behind me all the way. I finished year six at the age of eight and went straight to high school. By age 14, I finished and was out of high school. I immediately applied to a higher institution and got into college after my 15th birthday where I studied Computer Science. I did a two-year diploma there before going to medical school. By 23, I was a doctor.

Navigating Change (My Story)

Picture: My matriculation into College at the age of 15 – to study Computer Science, Yaba College of Technology

Picture: My matriculation into the University of Lagos at the age of 17 – to study Medicine and Surgery

Everything moved quite fast through school, but becoming a specialist always takes time. Despite moving to a different country and starting over again, I was a specialist by the ripe old age of 31. By 35, I had my Ph.D.

Navigating Change (My Story)

Picture: Ph.D. Graduation from the University of New South Wales, Australia, 2019

Academically, I was lucky to be gifted and so I never failed any exam. I had a retentive memory, and early on I realised that I was going to be a very academic person. I was not a hands-on person.

While there are other ways to uncover one's life purpose, I discovered my purpose through my academic prowess. I realised that I was good at complex reasoning, executing complex tasks, as well as analysing and understanding difficult concepts. That's why I'm a neurologist today. The brain is so complicated and I can understand the concepts enough to be able to help people with their brain disorders. There is also a part of me that is adept at critical reasoning. Despite having a very curious mind, I am always sceptical of any new idea. I never approach any idea with either disdain or overexcitement. Some people hear new quotes and are immediately mesmerised, but that isn't me. When I hear something, even if it is deep, I think through it, reflect upon it, and check it out. If it is true, I take it in. Even if it doesn't make sense, no idea is stupid to me. I'm still curious about wanting to understand why the person said what they said, or why people hold a certain point of view. So you see, my core values, natural abilities, and gifts pointed me towards what I am doing now. I knew I was going to be looking after vulnerable people and I thought my gifts were compatible with understanding the complex systems that revolve around people who are vulnerable or sick.

My external experiences also shaped my pursuit of purpose. One of the things I hate the most is seeing poverty because I have tasted poverty. I know what it means to wake up in the morning and have absolutely nothing to feed on. We had shelter, but we were absolutely poor. Seeing other people in vulnerable situations alongside my personal experience of being poor pushed me and gave me this drive for excellence. I wasn't going to settle for an average life because I had seen that and I had been there. I wanted something bigger. I decided that I am never, ever going to be poor again. Young and full of hope, I was determined to become a medical doctor. I knew that by doing this I would be able to fulfil my deep desire to help and care for people, using those internal instincts. Not only that, I knew it would break the cycle of poverty in my family. Even though I passed the university entrance examination in Nigeria, I could not get into medical school at the first attempt. Instead, I went to a college to study computing. I did my best and I got a distinction

Navigating Change (My Story)

in my last semester. When I got into college, I never gave up. My college fees were paid for by the church, primarily because my dad was not around and my mum had no money. I had just become a Christian and joined the church; in fact, I was a teacher in the children's department. The church just picked up the fees and helped me. That was when I learnt to just live by faith. I would wake up in the morning and go to school without any money. I often picked up a nylon bag, put my textbooks in it, and wrapped it all up. I still couldn't afford a school bag! As a university student, I would have to take two or three buses to campus. I didn't have any transport fare, so I would knock on the door of my neighbour, '*Mama Obe*', to beg for transport fare. What she gave me would only get me to the main terminal bus stop, still six kilometres from the campus. The fare for those buses would only allow me to stand; there were different fares for standing and sitting. So, after standing for about 30 kilometres, I would then walk for another six.

The first day I was able to afford a bike to peddle from the bus terminal to the campus, I shared a grateful testimony in the campus church group. That was just for transport. There was no breakfast, and lunch was by faith. I would trust God that I would eat that day. Sometimes, I would be dosing off in class, but I would do all the coursework for the lectures and trust God for a meal. Then, I would walk to the cafeteria by faith. Getting there, somebody somehow would bail me out. This went on for a whole year. One day, I got there and there was nobody in the cafeteria, so I walked up to the woman and told her that I was very hungry and had no money. I begged for food. In fact, there was a time I never ate breakfast for a whole year. But sometimes, we are hungry for more than just food, as this next story shows. Lectures were over on a warm breezy day, the whole campus bubbling with excitement and there I was, walking down the lane with another student. We were only a few blocks away from 'Hollywood' – a male hostel – when tragedy struck. Little did I know that the guy I was strolling with was about to give me the shock of my life. It was a moment to remember – an evening too many!

This guy was a dark-skinned young chap with a well-trimmed designer moustache and a trendy haircut that had fluttering waves like the readings of an abnormal electrocardiogram. He was tall and princely, well-built with muscles, and he walked with a celeb's gait. He was beautifully clad in an exquisite checked shirt matched with a pair of jeans and gorgeous urban sneakers. He talked with poise and elegance as he displayed his sparkling white teeth, well-arranged like a troop of marines on parade. With a very good carriage, his whole demeanour was very appealing. He also had an 'Americanised' accent that made him very humorous and much fun to be with. I was a sharp contrast to my colleague. I was not unkempt, but I did not have the charming privileges he had. I was vertically-challenged, lean, and reclusive in public circles (although I could be very playful when I was with my pals) I was also not confident to talk about my ideas in the open and I tried to hide this inferiority complex that haunted me. That day, I was dressed in an oversized, sagging purple shirt, with shoulder straps, making me look like an army cadet. With it was my undersized second-hand grey pants, which glowed in the sun – it had endured much suffering from ironing. It was a colour war, to say the least. To cap it all, I was wearing a rugged blue "KITO" sandal, which had served me for years with unquestionable loyalty – its threadbare sole was my witness. But it was not actually my fault – my wardrobe betrayed me! As we approached the hostel, my mate stopped suddenly and made a boisterous exclamation. It was as if a brilliant idea had just dropped into his analytical

Navigating Change (My Story)

mind. I turned to him, expecting to hear about his new brainchild, but alas, I was corrected! First of all, he did a critical craniocaudal assessment of my exterior and he sighed. He then opened his well-worn jaws and uttered a speech that was bereft of the slightest respect or pity. With a blunt effect, he told me that my outlook was loathsome and repugnant, and walking together with him was a huge embarrassment. And then, like a Ferrari, he zoomed off! And Jesus wept!

I stayed glued to my feet, my mouth gaping wide open with shock. It was a kick in the teeth, a blow below the belt, a knock-out punch. I was humbled, battered, and shattered. I felt like entering the ground. My heart haemorrhaged as his words raced through my mind again and again and again. *'He didn't even wait for an explanation'*, I muttered. That day, I prayed to God *never to be a poor man,* and I meant it. A war had begun! The die was cast! I would rather die fighting than be poor! That incident, about 20 years ago, changed my life and my mentality. Although it did lead to the demise of my beloved KITO. I still don't know how I managed to graduate with a distinction in my last semester. It was that challenging. I did not own a single textbook throughout that period, but I knew I had a desire to help people. Although I enjoyed computer programming, I still wanted to be in healthcare. I was just so passionate about doing something around the healthcare system. My purpose was still strong, so in my final year, I applied to go to medical school. I wrote the exam and was fortunate to be admitted. I remember praying to God and promising to scream 100 'Hallelujahs' if I got into medical school. Back then, the names of the successful applicants were published in some national newspapers which I could not afford to buy. So, my mum loaned some money from our neighbour.

Niyi Borire

I went to the newsagent, gave the man the money, and begged him to read the pages. When he opened it, I saw my name was seventh on the list. Keeping my promise, I went to church and there I shouted 100 Hallelujahs. I praised Him for being a covenant-keeping God. I finally studied medicine, which is what has got me to this point today.

Navigating Change (My Story)

Pictures: Graduation from the College of Medicine, University of Lagos in 2007 And Taking the Hippocratic Oath

Niyi Borire

My parents at my medical school Graduation ceremony – University of Lagos, Nigeria

So, my external experiences shaped my discovery of purpose. That's why, even though I had a distinction in computer science and could have followed that path, I was not fulfilled. That was not it for me. My fulfillment was from interacting with people. One other experience which shaped my life was when I was abused as a child. My wife only found out about this a few months ago. We lived in a two-storey building, where our flat was next to another flat. A woman whose age and face I cannot remember lived there. However, what she did to me that day is forever imprinted in my memory.

The lady was a house help for our neighbours. I was six years old. We were in the living room watching TV when she started touching me. At first, she touched me in a very unusual way. I never mentioned it to anyone, so I understand why people do not talk about their experiences with rape and abuse. I cannot forget it, even if I do not remember what she looks like. I remember we were on a mat and she covered us with a blanket so people thought we were sleeping. I was a child, but she was not. I remember her taking my hands and putting it in her private area and making me do things to her. I had no clue what that area was; I had never seen anything like that before. I remember that the following day, I went to my mum's room and she was asleep. I tried to check her to see what that area was. Up until now, my mum and I never spoke about it. I thought that she knew what I was doing because she just kicked the duvet and I ran out of the bedroom. I was so curious about where the lady had put my hands. I had never seen a female genital before then. Even though it may be different for a man, I understand how it can be difficult for women who go through sexual abuse to get over it. Many simply don't get over it.

The first time it became an issue for me was when I counselled a lady while I was the Youth President in church. I had just graduated from medical school. A lady in the church came to tell me she was just raped. I almost died, gasping for breath. Only later did I realise how exaggerated my reaction was. That was my first encounter with somebody who had been raped. The difficult family situation while growing up, along with my abuse experience which I couldn't talk about or mention to my parents because I did not think they would have believed me, all shaped my drive. If I had not cultured a positive approach, as detailed in the first chapter, I would have been a miserable and scarred person for the rest of my life.

Although it still hurts now and I cannot forget it or unlearn it, I think I have gotten over it. I still remember vividly what that lady did to me. Looking at where I am now, what made me today is all those failures and all that I went through. What has given me more robustness, a balanced outlook on life, empathy, and the legitimacy to reach out to people is the fact that I have been there too. That's why I can talk to a rape victim and give them comfort and hope. I have been there. That's why I can help people who are struggling and whose lives do not have meaning. There was a time I did not have any meaning. I cried all the time and used to ask God *why*. A good way to fulfil your purpose is to turn your hurts into other people's healing pills. Purpose can arise from curiosity about your life – the obstacles you have encountered, the strengths that helped you to overcome them, and how your strengths help make life better for others. As popularly said, when something bad happens, you have three choices. You can let it define you, let it destroy you, or you can let it strengthen you. Don't hate your past. No matter what it contained or what it did to you, the past shapes who you are, not just for the things you felt damaged you, but for the lessons you can take from it.

Lesson: What about your past makes you want a better future for yourself and others?

Chapter 3

Dreamer Boy

One fascinating thing about my childhood is that I was a dreamer boy. I like dreaming. Some may say it is a waste of time, but it was always a mental activity that I liked. It is probably one of my vices. Dreaming allowed me to release the creative and imaginative powers of my mind to paint a favourable picture of my future. It produced natural endorphins and hormones that made me feel good about myself. For a long time, it was my escape route. So, when things were not going well and there was nothing to do, I would go into that little corner. It was only a temporary escape, but it made me happy and I loved it. John Maxwell said, 'A dream is an inspiring picture of the future that energises your mind, will and emotions'. It is a picture of an inspiring future, not one that creates dread. It creates excitement and inspiration. I had many dreams, similar to Martin Luther King, who said, '*I have a dream that my four little children will one day live in a nation where they will not be judged by the colour of their skin but by the content of their character.*' That is from one of the most inspiring speeches ever written, one I used to know by heart. I read it so many times at the university. I've long had a dream of being able to communicate and affect lives. There is still a lot of growth I need to become a better communicator, but I had always dreamt of being able to inspire people, speak to affect their lives, and influence them positively. It has always been my dream to create positive change and bring that message of growing through change. At its heart is my driving force – to help people rise, change their position, and manage it in a way that will not be disruptive. For me, I always put myself vividly into the dream. There were many times I imagined how my wedding day would be. Even before I met my wife, I pictured myself there with a beautiful lady and how we would walk down the aisle.

There was a time I was so lost in thought while daydreaming that I was smiling on my own. My wife saw me and didn't understand what was going on, but I was laughing because of what I was daydreaming about. It made me feel good. Envisioning is important. In fact, someone once said, '*It's only the future that you can picture that you will feature*'. I had a lot of dreams and pictures I created in my mind about my future. One common picture I had then was being able to speak at an international event, standing before people of all races and colours to teach and tell them about original work. I have had this dream since I was a young man, but I had problems achieving that dream. The biggest difficulty was my inability to communicate.

As an adolescent, I was very shy in public. When I stood before a group, I would shrink and lose self-confidence. I felt I was more powerful on paper than in person. I could write emotive letters that would make people shake, but I did not have self-confidence while speaking in front of people. I eventually found

Navigating Change (My Story)

Ben Carson's book, *Gifted Hands*, which detailed his struggle in school as a child and how he was able to overcome it. That gave me faith and confidence that I could come out, be bold, and fulfil my dreams. But, it wasn't easy. I went to a public high school where we freely communicated in vernacular (even though we were officially supposed to speak English). This affected my ability to speak clearly and correctly and I often struggled with my tenses. But to fulfil my dream, I needed to be able to speak confidently.

I got comfort from learning about C.S. Lewis, one of the greatest writers of all time, who would always shrink before a crowd even though he had written some of the greatest books. In college, my colleagues and I would be talking about sports and then some of them would say things that were not factually correct. I would want to correct them, but I could not join the conversation. My heart would be beating erratically just due to a discussion because I was always scared of saying the wrong thing. I had low self-esteem because I could not communicate appropriately and surely.

Eventually, I decided to read books about speaking and listen to people who were good speakers. I soon gave my life to Christ, then joined the Bible study unit, where I was allowed to teach Bible study in a small class. I started teaching children's church; luckily those kids did not know the difference and could not pick any grammatical errors I made. That way, I put myself into an environment where I was teaching and speaking weekly. I started with those who were younger than me, then I moved on to adult Bible study, which gave me the confidence, strength, and encouragement to speak. When I got to medical school, we had to dissect cadavers in a neuroanatomy course. Before going to the laboratory, I would practise my speaking in front of the mirror. That preparation gave me confidence and made my group one of the best in the class. I applied myself, studying books (including the dictionary) to become a better speaker. Eventually, I got better and realised that I could engage the audience and communicate. Now, I communicate with my patients daily. I also counsel people and support them spiritually.

In 2017, while I was doing my Ph.D., I carried out a novel study on nerve damage in patients with kidney disease, which was then accepted by an international paper. I was nominated for the Golseth Young Investigator Award, a prestigious award for neurologists who care for patients that suffer from neuromuscular disease. I was astonished when they announced that I had won during the Neurologists' National Conference.

Picture: I won the Young Investigator Award at the Australian and New Zealand Association of Neurologists in 2015 – Auckland, NZ

I was flown to Phoenix, Arizona, and accommodated in a 5-star resort, where I stayed in their most luxurious suite. During the award ceremony in Arizona, I was called up to present my paper. As I walked up the podium to deliver a speech, I remembered how I had struggled two decades earlier. I remembered the times

Navigating Change (My Story)

I couldn't talk, the times I had ideas in class but I kept quiet because I was scared that I would make a mistake. Now, here I was, in front of a crowd mostly consisting of white men and women, clapping for me. My head swelled. I was so proud of myself. I walked up the staircase, smiling while looking at everyone. I stood before them and spoke eloquently about my original research and its findings. I was the third Australian ever to win this award since its inception. I was able to achieve this even though I was married, had children, was working as a neurologist, was serving in the church, had other responsibilities, and was a full-time student. I worked hard for the award. What was most striking to me was that I was able to stand in front of all those people, speak eloquently, and present my findings in a way that was succinct, efficient, timely, and captivating. Afterwards, a lot of people congratulated me; people I had never met before. There I was being celebrated at a global conference. Dreams come true. I could hardly believe that I was in America, presenting to an international conference with professors, talking about my original research! My brother, Gbenga, was getting married that weekend, so I only spent one night in Arizona before I joined him. When I was leaving, they gave me USD2000 in cash.

Picture: Presenting my research at Sydney's International Conference Centre in 2019

I also had a dream of being able to preach the word of faith, right from a young age. Earlier, I wanted to be an Anglican priest because I grew up in the Anglican church. There was a time I considered joining the Anglican church in Australia to become a priest. I soon realised the Anglican church here was different from the one I grew up in. Nonetheless, I had always dreamt that I would be able to speak into the lives of people and influence them for God. That mattered to me. I gave my life to Christ in August 1998, at a crusade. I listened to the Word. It was quite a shock to realise I had so many vices, including stealing and lying. I also mingled with bad friends. I don't know how I didn't get too tainted.

When I was in high school, I skipped quite a few classes, yet I was one of the best students. I would usually leave school to go to my friend's house, where we would watch movies. When I

Navigating Change (My Story)

got home, I would hang out with a different group of friends, who were intelligent and brilliant friends that I interacted with and shared notes with. So, there was always another way to compensate. When I gave my life to Christ, everything changed. I saw how I lived my life and decided to live for God. With this in mind, I wanted to make a difference in other people's lives, so I became a volunteer in the kid's church where I started to teach Sunday school classes. I felt (and still feel) that God had placed a calling on me to be a teacher of clear spiritual principles. That's one of the things I saw in myself very early on, but I had difficulty expressing and communicating that. It was my responsibility to develop my communication skills. That's why I have recently paid thousands of dollars to join the John Maxwell team so that I can become a better speaker and coach. That was one of my dreams that came to pass.

The bible says, *'Neither do they light a lamp and put it under a basket, but on a lampstand, and it gives light to all who are in the house. Let your light so shine before men, that they may see your good works, and glorify your Father in heaven'*. (Matthew 5:15-16 NKJV)

When I started at the medical school, I joined the campus fellowship and I became a volunteer. Soon after, I was invited to join the leadership team, occupying different positions throughout my time on campus. That was when my public speaking really kicked off. The more I spoke, the more I realised people were being blessed. I am now honoured to lead the Redeemed Christian Church of God (RCCG) Beautiful Gate, Sydney – a community church based in southwest Sydney.

When I see myself speaking before everyone, I remember the days when I had the dream of this. I remember being in a church admiring the preacher, hoping to one day speak like him and declare God's Word to others. I don't take it for granted now because it was always a dream of mine to be able to lead people the right way. I thank God because it proves that dreams come true. Another dream I had while growing up was to see my parents come to know the Lord. This was after I gave my life to Jesus. I knew that my dad was not born again, but he was extremely religious. He was an elder at the Anglican church that he attended and he was a member of the Parish Church Council, even though he knew he did not have a personal relationship with God. When his marriage broke down, my father went away to be with another woman, with whom he had two kids. I especially dreamt that my father would genuinely come to know the Lord. One day, I was alone praying in the church. I stood on the pulpit of the church and I prayed that my father would preach on that same pulpit. My dream was not just for my father's salvation, but that he would become a preacher. I went into the university chapel multiple times to pray for my parents' salvation. I pictured it as well. After the prayers, I would get back home and it would be chaos. There would be one problem or another. One day, I realised that I was using the wrong strategy. I was quite confrontational with my dad when I became older because I felt that he was not responsible – he was not paying my fees or giving us any money for food. After he left, my mum was left with five kids and no job, so she opened a small kiosk - just for subsistence. He still had a room in our three-bedroom house, so he would sometimes come back to take some of his things. During the week, I would pray and fast, but during the weekend when I crossed paths with my dad, it was confrontational. I could not get along with him. He was always there for us when we were much younger, and when he had the resources. However, after his business collapsed during my teenage years, a time when we were making big decisions about

Navigating Change (My Story)

our lives, he wasn't there. Not only that, I felt that he was punishing us because he wasn't getting along with our mum.

One particular day, a day I cannot forget because it was on my 17th birthday, I had just returned from a church conference and was home relaxing when my father came to the house with his friend. He called for a meeting with everybody, so we all sat down. He then announced that he intended to sell the three-bedroom apartment and had found a smaller one-bedroom apartment for us to stay in. He wasn't referring to my mum since they were not on speaking terms. My mum, looking at his friend, said she would sort herself out but she was not going to the one-bedroom flat. He then asked each of the five children what they wanted to do. One after the other, we replied that we were following mum. He then gave us until the 7th of January to move out. That meant we would have to pack throughout the new year to move out. Nobody said anything. I felt my father did not handle it properly because he took out all the pain he had towards his marriage on us. As he stood up to leave, I asked, *'Sir, can I say something? Sir, I know the reason why you are treating your family like this is because you have not known Jesus. I wish you would come to Jesus because if you do not, and you step out of that door and die, your blood will be on your head.'* It was the harshest statement I could have made, but I was angry.

My father lost it and wanted to jump on me. There was a big scuffle. Thank God he came with his friend, otherwise I don't know what would have happened. That was when our relationship hit rock bottom. I knew I had crossed the line, but I was really mad. This was a man who had been absent and was now willing to take the roof over my head. That ruined my birthday and I thought it was unfair in every respect. Still angry with me, his friend dragged him away. I felt remorseful the next day, but I could not speak to him. We didn't see each other for weeks. One day, I stumbled across my dad at a bus-stop. After he alighted from the bus, I did not greet him when he walked past. I ignored him because I felt he was dead to me at the time. That really pissed him off. Now that I am a father, I can imagine how much that would have stung. He came back to ask if I did not see him, but I continued ignoring him. He lost it and grabbed me by my shirt. People around began to beg him to stop, while I stood, speechless. He slapped me twice. Then I said, '*Don't slap me again*'. '*What will you do*'? he retorted. After the third slap, I punched him back. We fought. I had just attended a church service and there I was in a physical confrontation with my dad. I went back to commune with God, crying and praying about my indiscretion and the difficult situations which did not seem to be changing despite all my prayers. Life was a struggle and I was never happy. All this while, I had been praying for my dad, but my prayers and dreams were not a reality. There was a disconnect between my prayers and reality.

One day, on my way home from campus, I heard a terrible commotion while approaching the house. I knew something was wrong. Rushing into the house, I saw my father on top of my mum. They were both in their 50s at this time. When I saw my father punch my mother, I grabbed him by the neck and pinned him against the wall. He tried to push me away, but I was now bigger and stronger than him. I warned him, '*Don't ever touch her again*'. That was the last time I heard he touched my mum. He left, and I sank back into depression. I felt bad about what happened. I questioned why I treated him that way even though I was praying for his salvation. Later, I let it go. I stopped struggling to win an argument with him. When I graduated from medical school, he wanted to throw a party. I told him, '*Sir, you were not there most of the time. Now you want to pay for a party,*

Navigating Change (My Story)

but you did not pay for my school fees'. So, I said no to his plan. When this issue came up, my father reported me to the head of the church. He claimed that I tried to rob him of his honour as a father. They then called me from church and tried to persuade me to let him throw the party as my father. I eventually relented and allowed him to pay for the party, which was not what I wanted. While the other graduates celebrated in small tents with their families, my father paid for me to use one of the biggest university halls for the celebration. It was all for show.

My relationship with my dad was so low that when I became an adult, I still did not have a good relationship with him. When my father fell ill before he died, I talked to him about Jesus and he accepted Christ. Even though God answered my prayers, it was not in the way I wanted. When my father died, I cried. I reminisced on those days when I cried and prayed for God to save his soul. Even though I prayed for him back in those days when he was hitting me, I never gave up even when I wasn't seeing any sign of change. There were times that I misbehaved. There were times I lost it and hit him, but I still kept the dream in my heart. My father told me that he loved me for the first time a few weeks before he died. Lying there in hospital, sick, frail, and without a lot of energy, he relented. He mustered up all his energy, held my hand, and said, *'Niyi, thank you for all that you have done for me. I love you'*. But he had missed a lot of important events in my life. He did not see me get married. He did not see any of his grandchildren. He didn't really see me achieve anything. Sometimes, God does not answer our prayers in the way that we want, but I am grateful that my prayers were still answered. Although, he never climbed a pulpit to preach as I wanted.

Niyi Borire

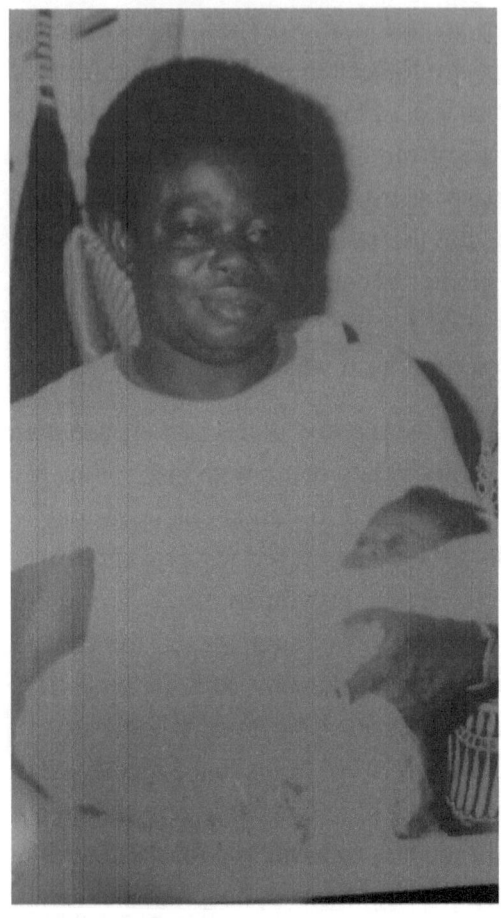

Picture: Dad and I at birth

Navigating Change (My Story)

Picture: Dad and I on my Graduation

In conclusion, dreams are very important. A dream is a picture of your future. I have found that when you have a picture of your future, it gives you guidance and energy. Eleanor Roosevelt said, *'The future belongs to those who believe the beauty of their dreams'*. When you have a dream that you believe in, it will always come to pass. God will always give you dreams that are bigger than your goals. God will never give you a dream that you can achieve on your own. If you can achieve it without support, it is no longer a dream. I had all those dreams because I could not do them on my own. I had a dream of speaking at a national conference when I had no bank account. I had nothing. I had no hope for the next meal, but I was dreaming that I would stand before an international conference to talk about my work

– and it came to pass. Plus, I had a dream that I would stand before the congregation of God and teach people, just like I am doing now. It was impossible then, but I had that dream. I had a dream that I would lead my father to Christ. That happened, but not in the way that I expected. And, it looked impossible. Even when I tried to reach out to him, there was no love there. I could not bring myself to love him, but I wanted him to see the light.

Picture: With Olayemi, my sweetheart

From that, I learnt that without love, our gospel is empty. Instead, I was releasing judgment on him. I saw him as not being good enough, as being irresponsible, and a failure. So, I judged him. I could not connect with love. I could not connect with him. Because there was no positive emotion, this killed my message. I could not convey the truth to him anymore. I tried to make that dream work by myself, but every time I tried, I failed. I would lose it, get angry, then regret it and sink into a mire of depression. Then, I would feel like God did not love me and everything was not working well.

Navigating Change (My Story)

My life is not perfect by any means, and all this has affected my family. My siblings are still not close to me. However, I'm still grateful because I know that I cannot have everything, but I love what I have now. My dream of having a peaceful home, I have that now. My wife may not be the perfect woman, but she is the woman for me, and we have worked hard for the last 11 years to make this marriage peaceful.

Dreams do come true.

Lesson: You picture yourself in your dream so you can believe it; but remember, you cannot do it on your own.

Chapter 4

Relationships

She asked, *'Who will you marry'*? I wondered why my mum would ask such a probing question from a young bloke like me. I replied briskly and said, *'I don't know who I will marry, BUT I KNOW WHO I WILL NOT MARRY'*. I will not marry a woman who does not have a place for God in her heart; a woman that will not love me for who I am; a woman who will neither have real delight nor pleasure in me; a woman that will not believe in the beauty of my dreams, however impossible they may appear; A woman that will not entertain the best opinion of my personality and actions; a woman that is too *'perfect'* to be improved or too *'seamless'* to be trimmed; a woman who is not sincere enough to tell me the truth when it would hurt; a woman that is not courageous enough to preach my sermons back to me; a woman that will not forgive my faults and understand my infirmities; a woman that will not protect me from shame and abuses; a woman that will not promote my spiritual, physical, and secular welfare; a woman that will not show me respect or honour; a woman that will not seek for my contentment and satisfaction; a woman without a voice or a

Navigating Change (My Story)

vision; a woman who does not invest, but wants to harvest; a woman who does not originate, but only manipulates; a woman without convictions or standards; a woman who can easily be bought with a prize and swayed with currency; a woman who is ashamed of what is right because it is unpopular; a woman who cannot say an emphatic NO to evil because the whole world says YES"! I thought it would be almost impossible to find such a blessed woman, free of these failings. But, I was dead wrong. There are so many wonderful women out there waiting to be wanted. It is the glory of God to conceal a 'wife'; it is the honour of kings to search her out. Thank God, I found mine – the woman of my dreams! Though imperfect, yet altogether virtuous – what a paradox! – my wife, Olayemi, is my life partner.

Relationships make or break a man. Over the years, I have had some wonderful relationships which have made remarkable changes in my life. The first and most important one is my marriage. Developing a strong bond of friendship has been the mainstay of our relationship. We share similar values and world view, and we accept each other for who we are as individuals. Friendship is important with a life partner. Olayemi and I met in church and we were friends, but back then, I never thought about her in a romantic way. Olayemi and I were in the same writers' group where we wrote articles for the church. I knew she liked me, but it was not unusual for me to get attention and I wasn't really keen. Eventually, I started getting text messages from her. She seemed to know I was going to be her husband before I knew and she strategically positioned herself in my sphere of influence. She saw me in her life even before we dated, as she sent me curious, strategic messages from time to time. She let me become curious: who was this girl?

We met in church and we started connecting. She was very open and she really liked me. Olayemi had bow legs, which were initially a turn-off. Attraction is really important. I prayed about it and realised that our friendship had grown. I did not hear a voice from God; I just had pure, divine, inspired love for her. This was deep. Very quickly, I began to see her in another light. The physical deformity of her legs did not bother me anymore. I started to see her beautiful face, her smell, and everything else about her. Physical attraction is really important in a relationship. There has to be some form of physical attraction.

Indeed, I was attracted to her, but there was much more. She grew on me and the love blossomed in my heart. It was not a lustful desire. I knew it was different. I knew God had put the love in my heart because when I prayed about it, I felt peace in my heart. We gave it time and it grew and blossomed. We didn't rush it. When I was with her, there was no impure desire. There was just pure, unadulterated love for her. I shared my feelings with my mentors and they prayed with me.

Getting our parents on board was difficult. My father did not approve until the time he died. My mum did not approve initially either, but I made her realise that she had to. I guess they were initially bothered by her bow legs. Initially, my wife struggled academically. She had low self-esteem, she had bow legs and she used to tell me that she never knew any man who would marry her. Despite her pain, I was attracted to her attitude, character, and smile. I was physically attracted to her despite her bow legs. It was a divine and inspired love. I felt it stronger and stronger. My parents were initially sceptical, hoping that I would marry one of my doctor friends. They were not expecting me to be with somebody from our church. Even the chaplain was surprised, but I stood my ground and made it very clear that it was what I wanted. It took a while for my mum to come around, but my father never had the chance. During the time my father was sick, my wife's caring attributes shone and my mum quickly realised she was a good woman. Ultimately, it worked out well, but I would have married my wife anyway.

The day I proposed to her, I was in her house and she asked me if I wouldn't ever propose to her. I thought our relationship was already so deep that she did not require a formal proposal to know my commitment to her and our future. I didn't have money, a ring, or anything. Right there and then, I knelt, gave her my Bible, and asked her to marry me. That same week, it dawned on me that I needed to make my feelings known, and so I wrote her a romantic letter that swept her off her feet.

26th June 2007

Sweet,

Right from the last month of the year 2004, my love for you has been growing in geometric proportions. This culminated in an event which took place on the 12th of May this year when I made a formal proposal to you. I can still remember vividly the radiance that beamed out of your face. It pierced my heart like the surgeon's scalpel. I was flooded, inundated, and overwhelmed with a barrage of irresistible passion. I felt masculine. I felt mature.

Here was a young man under the captivating spell of a romantic, sweet, tender feminine voice saying: 'I will ...I will marry you, Monsieur Niyi'.

It was as if I was stung by a bee. 'If this is a dream, may I not wake up. If this is what psychiatrists call psychosis, let me not recover'! At last, I have been initiated. I can walk with my head raised high because I've caught a fish. Not just any, I made a big catch - Bill Gates can't even afford her price!

Olayemi, it's 2:35 a.m. I am writing this note this morning to confirm my relationship with you. Attached to this letter is a copy of the Holy Writ. I do not know of any better token that can serve as the seal of our relationship. A diamond ring will not do. Never! Only God's infallible word can serve as the relic of our engagement.

With this Bible, I engage you as my only darling.

With this Bible, I engage you as my love, my sweetheart.

With this Bible, I engage you as my fiancée, my future wife.

With this Bible, I engage you as my companion, mother to my unborn kids.

With this Bible, I engage you as my fellow soldier and partner in ministry.

I will love you as this Bible teaches.

I will honour you the way this Bible admonishes.

I will give you my undivided affection as this Bible commands.

This is our charter, our constitution, our creed!

I take you this day as my future bride, my blue-eyed princess, my fair-haired queen, my heartthrob.

Behold, thou hath fair my love thou hast ravished my heart, my sister ... my dove, my undefiled ...

Set me as a seal upon thine heart, as a seal upon thine arm: for love is as death... many waters cannot quench love, neither can floods drown it!

Navigating Change (My Story)

Love from yours,

Niyi

I made promises in that letter which I am still fulfilling today. As our relationship evolved, Olayemi was 'all-in'. Our dates were spent studying the Bible together and I loved impressing her with my quotes. Afterwards, we would go to her house to eat. Towards the end of our courtship, most of her savings were spent on me. She saved money for me, not herself.

Commitment is key. We committed to each other and I told everyone about her. Once I knew exactly what I wanted, there was no looking back – we just began to build together. We had nothing but ourselves and our dreams. We met together to pray, study the Word, and for fellowship. We talked about our family and future kids. We talked about our future – she knew my plans to travel overseas. She knew I was driven, so she was committed too. She believed in my dreams. We prayed about it and kept going.

We are a very good team, in fact, I can't remember any arguments. We made a covenant from the beginning that our relationship was non-negotiable. We were confident about the decision we made together. We were both convinced. By the time I proposed to her, we both knew what God wanted for us.

Commitment means working through differences. We made a covenant to resolve any issues that would arise without disrupting the relationship as a whole. We had a few differences that we were able to work through because we loved each other beyond any fault. We were ready to make it work.

I went to visit Olayemi on her birthday, with a letter to her in my pocket. When I entered the door, her mum hugged me and thanked me for the beautiful gift. I was so confused. I played along, even though I did not know what was going on. After getting into the house, Olayemi brought out a beautiful pair of shoes that I definitely could not have afforded. I was scared because I did not understand where she got the money to buy the gift. Everybody was gushing over the shoes, and I was feeling special. When everybody calmed down and left, she explained to me that she bought them as she was not happy. She did not want things to be awkward again that year, so she bought the gift herself on my behalf. That day, I knew I would marry her. A bonus was, for the first time, everybody treated me with much respect.

One good aspect is that her parents loved me from the start and I did not have any issues with her own family. Her dad might call me at 2 a.m. just to tell me that he loves me. All my friends became her friends and vice versa. We shared activities and became close to her family. Her house was my second house. Her mum bought several provisions and appliances for me to take to school then. I became a member of her family.

When we were first together, we had mentors. Mr. Awe was close to us. We did everything together under his leadership and mentorship. I informed him when I wanted to take Olayemi on a date to the beach, which would have required three buses from my house. I was so excited that I did not consider the stress that would have been involved with transporting all our beach gear between the buses. Mr. Awe made me realise the date would have been messy for her and she would not have been treated right. He advised me not to do it. Initially, I regretted telling him about it, but I listened and then asked her if we could hang out in church instead. His advice was good and reasonable. I did not

Navigating Change (My Story)

have a car, so there was no way to make it work. That kind of conversation with our mentors kept us grounded. There was a time that I was not listening much and Olayemi spoke to Mr. Awe about it. He called me and taught me the art of negotiation and patience.

Before travelling to Australia, my mom insisted that I marry Olayemi at the registry in Nigeria, which I did.

Niyi Borire

Pictures: At the Marriage Registry with my wife in Lagos, Nigeria – January 11, 2009

One of the most difficult times I had maintaining purity was when she visited me in Australia a few months later. We had both agreed that we would keep ourselves pure until our wedding night, but it was difficult for me. I had to wait for three months until we had our wedding in Newcastle, NSW (even though we were already legally married). Our journey up to that wedding was great, and we continued building after that. She is the best thing that has ever happened to me. She's very understanding, mature, and caring. She prays for me and corrects me. We're a good team.

Picture: Our wedding day in Australia

Relationship building starts with friendship, compatibility, and covenant. We worked on our strengths, minimised our weaknesses, were open to each other, worked together, and suffered together. She initially wanted to study law, but I encouraged her to study nursing and she agreed for the sake of the family. Now, she's in law school, studying what she wants to. She sacrificed so that I could succeed in my career. She sometimes had to take our son to work at night with her, but she never argued or complained. She understood and we worked together.

I didn't take her for granted or make it all about me either. When we were dating, I travelled to wherever she was to see her, even if I had to borrow money for transport fare. I made it work, and when it was her turn, she also made it work. There is absolutely nothing she wants that I cannot give to her (that is within my power) because she has repeatedly shown that she is a selfless person and she believes in me.

My Mum and my Siblings

My mum, Christiana, is a warrior. She is fierce, yet friendly. She is sacrificial, yet she can keep you in line. She is incredibly kind and can be everything at the same time. She can be kind and friendly, yet firm. She is very opinionated, independent, and will never allow anyone to walk all over her. I inherited that independent trait from her.

Niyi Borire

Picture: My Mum, Christiana Oluremi Borire

She never loses an argument. Till now, I have never won an argument with my mum. She cannot be pinned down. She never gives up. That can be both good and bad. When she had the chance to walk away from her marriage, she stood firm and fought for it. She took all the blows, aches, disappointment, and pains. Even when she had no job, she went to the abattoir to get scraps from cows, goats, and lamb to sell to feed her 5 children. She sold her clothes and possessions to keep a roof over our

Navigating Change (My Story)

heads. Like a mother lion, she went to any extent to fight for her kids, defend their honour, and provide for them. She never gave up. Even with all their physical fights, she never surrendered to my dad. With her bloodied face and bruised body, she would scream and fight back. She was a tiger! She still is.

In hindsight, it is not my place to judge or comment on what role her strong personality had on her marriage because I have never been in her shoes. What I can say is that she fought very hard for her marriage, no matter how tough it got. My father came back home before he passed away. Even though it was difficult, my mum still had the heart to forgive him. Even though he left the marriage and had two kids with another woman, my mother did not push him away when he returned. She let him back in. Not only that, she nursed him during his illness until the time he passed. For three whole months, she visited him in the hospital every single day, no matter how exhausted she was. She looked after him, cared for him, and loved him. Even though there was no more romance, there was still affection. Even though they were old and frail and so much had changed, she still showed up for him.

One may argue that her strong-willed nature is the reason for our strained relationship, but ultimately that's who she is. She is authentic, real, and brave. She did not shy away from her responsibilities and she was always ready to go the extra mile. She stood by her kids, provided for them, and never left.

Initially, mum and I had a great connection, but the relationship did not progress as I got older. This had nothing to do with my mum or her personality. She didn't do anything to create a distance. If anything, she made efforts to reach out to me, but I struggled to be comfortable in that chaotic environment. I felt there was too much drama going on at home and found it very overwhelming. It was difficult for me to connect with everyone, particularly my siblings, not just my mum. I was unhappy and struggled with my insecurities. I felt life could be better and I did not know how to deal with that as a child.

Since I did not know how to cope, I essentially ran away from home. I felt more comfortable being away from home, and I thought the distance would help, but on reflection, I don't think it did. The distance did not change my reality. Although I felt more comfortable being away, it did not help my relationship with my mum or my siblings.

Picture: With my siblings

My siblings are very special people. My sister, Funke, is one of the sweetest human beings you will ever encounter. She has a larger-than-life personality. She is full of love and hope. Simply, she is awesome. She has had her fair share of challenges and disappointments in life, but she is also a fighter. I see in her the determination to overcome her current challenges day by day.

Navigating Change (My Story)

My brother, Gbenga, is a really good guy. He is a much better giver than I am, to the extent that he has gone into debt just to help other people out. Like Funke, he is also a fighter. He has had a lot of difficulties, but he kept going. He found the love of his life and they now have a beautiful son together.

I really admire Gbenga and Funke for their determination. Even though we don't have the kind of relationship I would have liked, we get along quite well. I was not around most of the time, which ultimately affected my relationship with my siblings. We didn't have enough time to bond, hang out, and get to know each other. I don't know what our relationships would have been like had we spent more time together and built the connection, but we do have a relationship. I'm sure we could have achieved a lot more together if we had developed that connection.

Omolara is the baby of the house and she is a treasure. Rumour has it that she came by surprise. She sacrificed a lot just to be there for my mum. She is the closest to mum. She is just a delightful person and a pleasure to have as a sister.

My other sister, Sola, is fiery! I believe she inherited a double portion of mum's toughness, but she is still a sweetheart. She can be as boisterous as a raging bull, yet as calm as a dove.

***

My First Coach

There is a difference between being a counsellor, mentor, or coach. A counsellor listens and imparts knowledge to someone else. A mentor shares their own experiences. If I am mentoring you, you will have to assume that I have gone through what you are about to go through now. I will share my experience with you to build competence. On the other hand, a coach does not share knowledge or experience. A coach asks questions to draw out hidden gems and ideas in you, to improve your performance.

The job of a coach is to build up your vision and dreams. Unlike a teacher or mentor, who is meant to load you with what you don't have, the job of a coach is to let you see what you already have and give you a sense of self-awareness. A coach will help you to know who you are, what strengths you have, and help you to maximise your productivity. Counsellors and mentors produce competence; coaches improve performance.

Christian Simpson, a world-renowned coach said, *'Coaching is inside out, not outside in. It helps the participants realize the potential they have on the inside of them. It helps to create greater awareness, increase responsibility, and develop accountability. Coaching is geared towards improving performance'.* Coaching fills the gap between what a person knows and what a person does and it helps make them accountable.

The story of my life would not be complete without Ayodele Awe. He is not just somebody I look up to – he was my very first coach. Mr. Awe never shared his experiences with me, but he was very good at listening, asking me questions, and helping me to see the depth and breadth of my strength and capacity. Even though people saw me as a natural leader, I still had an inferiority complex. He helped me to see the best in me; to see that I was valuable, talented, and could achieve anything I wanted to.

Shortly after my dad left home, I went to his office because I needed to pay my school fees for my first year in medical school. He told me he couldn't help me. His business was paralysed and he was struggling. I was expecting to get some assurance that we could work something out eventually, but he just told me point blank that he could not help. I knew he was also transferring

Navigating Change (My Story)

some of his ill-feelings about my mum to me. I thought this was unfair, so I walked out of his office feeling sad and miserable.

The following Sunday, I was teaching in the children's church. I was enrolled in college, but taught in the children's church whenever I visited home. After I taught the high school class and we finished the service, I let my guard down. I stayed in one corner of the hall, feeling down. Mr. Awe, once my teacher in high school, came over and asked why I was sad. I did not want to talk, but he encouraged me to open up. When I shared the situation with him, he told me with a steely-eyed look that I was not going to stop medical school. That very week, he paid my fees. In fact, he paid every single fee until I graduated medical school. He even bought my flight tickets to Australia.

We're not related, but this man was there for me. He coached me. He also allowed me to stay at his house while I was not happy living at home. It was peaceful. I became involved with his family. In coaching me, he built me up.

Picture: With my mentors, Mr. & Mrs.. Awe. This man paid my way through Medical School.

Friendships

Over the years, I have had friends who helped me get to my goals. I have leaned on their wisdom, knowledge, and experience to build my life to where I am now. Some people lose their friends when they find their life partner. That is a very asymmetric way to view relationships. A lot of people succeed in one area (like business) and lose in another (like their love life). If you marry somebody that will disconnect you from your roots, your family, or your friends, watch out! You are looking for trouble. Generally, somebody who is a life partner who really loves you will also love your friends. Of course, they will also help you to prune out friends, but if you are losing all of your friends just because of your life partner, then you need to be wary. Having that balance of a network of people with whom

Navigating Change (My Story)

you share a similar goal and passion and who push you is important.

It is good to have romantic relationships and be committed to somebody that you can love unconditionally, but it is also good to have friends that can build you up, challenge you, and inspire you to stretch yourself. It is also good to have mentors who you can be accountable to, and who will challenge you and pick you up.

Friends are also important because they often add, not subtract. Sometimes, friends don't see our full selves. They see our front side and help us to put on more make-up. They don't see the dark spots on your back that your partner will see. Friends add virtue and improve what they see. So, mingle and have relationships with people who have value. Friends add value to us, whereas our life partners not only add value, they also seek to remove things that should not be there and direct our eyes towards our deficiencies.

Having somebody like a mentor to be accountable to, be open and vulnerable to, is important. Mentors cut across multiple areas; as a doctor, I have professional mentors; I have family friends who are mentors, and I have spiritual leaders who are mentors. Every successful person should have robust relationships across the board.

The most important thing about mentorship is accountability. A mentor will challenge you and take you up to a higher level. They can bring out the best in you and help you to achieve what you want to achieve. Oftentimes, they have been through what you have been through, so they can give advice.

A good mentor will not lay down their own experience as the gospel and insist that you follow their ways. A good mentor will give you principles that transcend time and culture; principles that will give you good results when applied to your life.

The beauty of life lies not just in being good in one area but having balance. A balanced life is a successful and robust life. Some of my colleagues are excellent in their career, but they are not happy in their relationships. That's because there is no balance. Even in a relationship itself, you need to have balance – balance with friends, your network, mentor(s) and your life partner.

You Need an Apollos

Paul planted, Apollos watered, but God gave the increase (1 Corinthians 3:6-7, NKJV).

No man has a monopoly on knowledge. No matter how blessed you are, a few things in your life will be lacking. Our lives are like smartphones – no matter the brand you're using, another phone will have a feature that yours is missing. There is no complete package. There is something about you that somebody else is better than you at – it could be intelligence, skill, etc. That is reality. Understand the fact that we live in a defective world and we are defective – whether in our emotions, feelings, discipline, or in the way we think and see things.

Sometimes, our understanding of our identity is influenced or affected by our culture. We can sometimes judge ourselves based on our culture – our childhood, value system, exposure, and experiences. They all help us to define ourselves. Friendship is an experience we have that helps us to define and find ourselves and understand our place in the world. Without true friendship, it is difficult to have the robustness that will help us to achieve what we need to achieve.

Navigating Change (My Story)

Paul might have planted the seed, yet he needed someone else to water it. In our lives, we need people. Some of us are blessed with certain gifts and seeds which we can plant, but we need other people to water the seeds so that God can give the increase. Sometimes, we are the ones watering the seed that others have planted. Ultimately, God gives the increase but there are many times where we may not be able to water the seeds we have already.

My First Friend

A very good friend of mine in high school, Folusho, created one of the deepest impressions in my heart. He was my destiny helper. We were so close; age mates in the same class. We could speak at the same level, no matter what we were talking about. We had a lot in common, but we could also challenge each other. We would pick abstract concepts, opposing views, and just argue it out. Nobody won, but we stretched each other. Each of us rarely gets offended, and if we do, we discuss it straight away. We had a great connection, often holding hands while walking on the street. We both loved to express our feelings. We had high regard for and we loved each other.

Back then, he was training to be a chartered accountant, while I was still studying computing. We would sit at the bus-stop together after college and we would sing acapella together. We brought our families together by visiting each other often. We later became close covenant friends. When I gave my life to Jesus, knowing Folusho made a lot of difference. It helped me with the foundation because he also loved God. He gave his life to Christ a few years before me.

The day he had doubts in his heart about God, he came to me. That was just before the time I also had doubts. He cried, and I encouraged him in response. A few months later, I was in that place of doubt too; we encouraged each other. We always had each other's backs. It was a great connection and friendship.

Folusho eventually went for his professional exams, which he passed with good grades. He had a First Class Bachelor's Degree, then went to do his MBA. He is now a chartered tax agent, accountant, and much more. He has a beautiful wife and three lovely kids now. He is also a great writer. Back then, he wrote different Christian materials which I then reviewed. With so much in common and him helping my Christian faith, my relationship with Folusho became one of the most important in my life. We built each other up in the faith and we always had a deep connection.

Another important friendship I had was with Busuyi, my roommate at university. He was much older than me and very grounded. We had a very good bond and he supported me. He was also very influential in my growth in ministry – I learnt so many things with him.

My true friends were very passionate people. They pushed me to study. We were just hungry. I never had friends that would settle for less. Friends like Busuyi did not want an average life. They wanted more, and they wanted to succeed. I was attracted to that and that helped me flourish. I learnt a lot from this good friend of mine who built me up.

There was a day I was on the edge of compromise; I wanted to make a decision that would have compromised my Christian stand, but Busuyi saved me. I was in my fourth year of medical

Navigating Change (My Story)

school when I became close to one of my classmates, a lady. There was no doubt we liked each other, but despite our closeness, we defined our relationship as mere friendship. There was nothing romantic. But good things can become corrupted when lines are crossed. We got too close and I became emotionally attached, even though God had already told me the lady I was going to marry did not attend my university. To summarise the ordeal, I opened up to my good friend, Busuyi. He supported me and advised me to stay away from her. I realised that I had become too self-confident and I was losing my focus. I wasn't as devoted as I used to be. I could still preach and people would commend me, but I knew I was losing the basis of my Christian faith. Busuyi prayed with me and I rededicated myself to God. I had to step down from my religious responsibilities to focus on my rehabilitation.

I learnt a big lesson from this experience. So many people are currently in relationships that they are not fully aware of. They may think it is friendship, but it is much more. Sometimes, relationships that are not meant to be can morph into things that are bigger than us.

Picture: With my best mate in College, Busuyi Alabi.

Lesson: I became who I am today because of the quality of my networks and friendships. All my life, people have been my greatest assets. You can barely achieve anything significant without people. You need people. In fact, people constitute the greatest asset on the path to success.

Chapter 5

Integrity

My definition of integrity is: standing upright no matter what. It does not connote a lack of weakness or flaws. A person of integrity is one who is so flawed and so weak but has learnt to lean on or leverage supporting structures. To be a person of integrity means a person has found a way to link his personality with a higher power and link himself to other people who will keep him accountable. You can be a weak and flawed person and still be a person of integrity if you learn how to be vulnerable before God and depend on Him to strengthen you. You also need to learn to lean on other people's strengths and experiences. The law of leverage means that you can use a lever to lift a big box that you cannot lift on your own.

To stand upright, we need to use our faith and what we have as leverage to tap into all that we do not have. Leaning out, asking for help, and being vulnerable is one of the best ways to overcome. A man or woman of integrity is not one who cannot fall; a person of integrity has learnt how to leverage their relationships to stand – relationships with God and fellowmen.

The four temperament model categorises people into four personality groups namely: choleric, sanguine, phlegmatic, and melancholic. My temperament type is a combination of sanguine and choleric. My choleric side is that I am a born leader. I'm a visionary. No matter how exhausted I am, I don't stop until I have completed what I need to do. I have strong leadership qualities, which sometimes make me insensitive to other people, but on the positive side, I have to accomplish my goals. I do not settle for less.

My sanguine side is more playful and doesn't usually come out in public. When I am in my element, I am a cheeky prankster. The sanguine aspect of my temperament makes it difficult for me to keep secrets, but fortunately, pastoring has helped me to learn how to. Responsibility stretches a person, as it did me. One of the reasons my relationship with my wife is so good is because she knows almost everything; I keep no secrets from her. Despite our individual flaws, we have learnt to adapt and communicate with wisdom.

My personality has made me pre-disposed to certain weaknesses. While I have many talents, academically brilliant, and having experienced several successes, I have experienced the highs and lows.

After I gave my life to Christ, I was caught in a web of masturbation. Those nights, I cried and prayed for God to help me. I had never touched a woman before. I cannot remember exactly how it started, but it became a struggle. I was a worker in the fellowship and would sometimes have 'good' days. I

Navigating Change (My Story)

would be okay for months, then something would happen to trip me up. It was emotionally draining. I prayed, I engaged in marathon fasting, and I memorised and meditated on scriptures. I could have months of victory before something would trip me up and I would relapse. I kept stumbling and falling. Then, I had a reputation of being a 'spirit-filled', 'tongue-speaking' brother. It was hard. The cycle continued until I opened up to my accountability partner. I told him I was struggling. I remember we prayed and sought the face of God. That was my first sustained and consistent victory.

After I got married, it tried resurfacing. Thank God for my wife; now it's my past, but it very easily could have still been my predicament. My wife played a big role and even became my accountability partner. I installed a software programme called 'Covenant Eyes' on all our devices, which blocked unnecessary sites and notified my wife if I visited any website I shouldn't have. I opened up to her and she prayed. This experience made me realise that marriage does not change the urge to masturbate. When I experienced a relapse after marriage, it wasn't from a lack of sex. You can have sex regularly and pornographic images will still appeal to you. My wife was determined to help break the habit. She held me accountable and I was vulnerable, which was very important.

I'm a flawed man, but I leveraged my relationships with God and people to stand strong. I don't know how God kept me from any scandal, even though there were many opportunities. There is a restraining grace of God upon my life that kept me from certain things. I really struggled with masturbation, but God gave me victory. Now, it is a testimony that I can share to inspire others. I am unsure if the lustful curiosity I had may or may not have been linked to the sexual abuse I experienced when I was younger. Nonetheless, I realised that there is no height someone can get to that they cannot fall from. That was the lowest point of my spiritual walk with God.

Integrity does not mean flawlessness, it means standing up for what is right despite our flaws, and learning to use our relationships as leverage to stand upright. No matter how high one goes, no human being can ever get to the point of infallibility. Every human being is flawed. We have weaknesses in our personalities that expose us and make us vulnerable to compromise, so we need to lean on God's grace and have accountability partners to help us. I've heard people try to normalise masturbation and the guilt that comes with it, but it is an abnormal expression of sexuality.

I believe that 'virginity is dignity and not just a lack of opportunity'. My wife and I had several opportunities during our courtship, but we made the decision that we wanted integrity in our courtship and she held me accountable for that. Till now, she stabilises me and balances me. Even though I am a flawed person, I have learnt to leverage my relationships to build my strength.

A few situations have challenged my integrity in life. The first one I remember was when I applied to college to study computer science. I decided to use a fake birth certificate because I did not meet the minimum age requirement for entry into college. The birth certificate I used for the application added five years to my actual age. A few years later, I learnt about restitution, so I went back to college to confess what I had done. I expected them to nullify my degree, so I was surprised that they accepted my apology. Afterwards, I showed them my real birth certificate.

Navigating Change (My Story)

Another time I struggled with integrity was when I was in my second year of medical school, studying biochemistry, a course that had a practical component that required a logbook. I made a photocopy of a logbook because I could not afford to buy the original. The photocopy was done so well that nobody but me knew it was not the original book. The only way anybody would have known was by checking the master list, which detailed those who purchased a logbook. At the end of the year, we had a practical exam and they asked us to produce our logbooks. Since I did not have an original one, I threw my fake logbook into the garden outside. I was the last one to enter the exam hall. When asked about my logbook, I apologised and said I had left it in my room in the hostel. Luckily, they still allowed me into the exam hall, but I felt guilty for lying. A few weeks after the exam, I felt convicted in my heart to make my ways right. I promised God that I would tell them I lied after the results were out, but God said I had to go before the results were released. I took a bold step to apologise and tell the head of the biochemistry laboratory why I was unable to purchase the original logbook. She felt bad that I did not tell the truth initially. For almost a month, I had been living under the guilt of what I had done. The moment I confessed, a weight was lifted off my chest. I decided that next time, I would stand and say the truth. Integrity really matters.

Those experiences, as seemingly trivial as they were, showed me that sometimes our worst fears do not exist – they are an illusion. Sometimes, we are scared to say the truth because it is not popular or may lead us into trouble. We must learn to lean on His grace, be truthful, honest, and do what is right. It may cause displeasure and initially produce pain, but it is better than being phony, hypocritical, and lying.

My own experiences with integrity have taught me to make restitution when I do wrong. It is important because it creates credibility and you pay forward – you open doors in the future. Some of the restitutions I have made in the past have taught me to open up. If you need help, come out and ask for it. If you do not ask for help, there is no way you can receive it.

Be open, vulnerable, and sincere for change. I have learnt that if you have an addictive sin, you cannot just pray about it. For healing to take place, you need *insight* and *sincerity*. A man who is mentally ill, but does not know he is sick and runs away from a cure, lacks insight. He lacks self-awareness because he does not know his true state. If he knew his true state, he would run to God for healing. The man who is sick but pretends not to be sick lacks sincerity. This also happened in the case of Samson in the Bible. He was married, but he was caught with another woman. In order to escape, he rose from the bed of adultery and carried the gate of the city (which ordinarily, 50 men would not have been able to lift) to the top of the hill. The perfume of the harlot had not left his body. He stood up from the bed and still used his strength, as he had prior. Samson was not sincere. Perhaps, he lacked insight and thought things would just work, but he had forgotten the covenant he made.

Sincerity is important if you're going to be a person of integrity. You must understand yourself, your frailties, and your weaknesses, then lean on your relationships (with God, your mentors, and your accountability partners) to help you build your integrity. During my rehabilitation, I learnt that every single day you overcome is a good day for you. Now, masturbation is a thing of the past, something I have learnt to deal with. Based on my conditioning and strength, the urge is no longer there. Every battle you win gives you strength and confidence for future battles. That is one thing I have learnt.

Another time my integrity was tested was when I travelled to South Africa during my time in medical school for an elective exchange programme. I got to Pretoria by the grace of a stranger but the programme was set to take place at Stellenbosch University in Cape Town. Being a long, long way still, I did not have enough money to get to Cape Town even though I had already obtained my South African short-stay visa. So, I ended up going to Pretoria, where I met a few friends.

While I was in Pretoria for four weeks, I realised there was a scheme going on amongst the migrant community – many of them were getting arranged marriages. The choirmaster of one of the local churches I attended, and my temporary host, was part of the scheme. He introduced me to the scheme to marry me to a South African girl so I could get a right to stay, then a permanent residency. It would be just a formal arrangement and not a relationship and we would get a divorce a few years later. All of this was to be arranged for me in absentia. I was supposed to send my passport and other required documents via mail when I returned to Nigeria. After arranging everything, they would then send a 'partner's visa' for me to return to South Africa. I was being swayed by the opportunity to live in a beautiful country, with working electricity, running water, and many work opportunities. That year, I won a scholarship and everything seemed to line up. The exact value of the scholarship was the exact amount that I needed for the scheme. I thought it was a great coincidence and I was sold. The positive experience and observations I had during my visit further inspired me to migrate to South Africa after medical school. I schemed, planned, and made up my mind to send the money and the necessary documents to get it done. That was my secret plan. My scholarship fund came through when I returned to Nigeria. I tried to justify the fact that the person who introduced me to the scheme was a Christian, but I knew it was wrong. It was wrong, but I just wanted a break. I wanted to take a chance.

For about a month, the scheme laid heavy on me, so I decided to open up to a friend. I called him one day, told him about the scheme and that I was about to send money for it. He told me I could not do it because I was a Christian. That was all I needed to hear. The scales immediately fell off my eyes. I could not believe I had even considered it. We prayed and I felt different immediately. The drive, pull, and attraction all disappeared. I would have been trapped because that would have officially been my first marriage. It would have been a big mistake.

Another temptation of my integrity loomed large when I got to Western Australia, alone but already married. I could not get a job after passing my exam and my three-month tourist visa was about to expire. I met a much older woman at an event and we started chatting. She was probably in her 40s and she lived alone. I knew she was interested in me, so she seemed to be the fastest way for me to get permanent residency. At that time, I was at my wit's end, without a job, and my visa was almost expiring. I was desperate. It crossed my mind to break my wife's heart. I went to my bag, took out our marriage certificate, and told myself it was the most stupid thing I had ever done. How could I have gotten married? I felt trapped. I felt that if I had come to Australia as a single person, it would have been easier to date and marry somebody else, a citizen.

Eventually, I saw sense and I strategically withdrew from the situation. She was a nice lady who was lonely and needed companionship, but I knew she wasn't for me. The next day, I

Navigating Change (My Story)

told my wife about it. She may have freaked out internally, but she thanked me for letting her know. She knew I would not have told her if I was actually planning to do it.

Lesson: Integrity is what keeps you on track even when the prying eyes of the world are not on you. It is what makes you do the right thing. Integrity is based on sincerity and insight. I have learnt that integrity is the foundation of a truly successful life. As it is often said, power will take you to the top, but character will sustain you there.

Chapter 6

Exploits of Faith

———————⪼●⪻———————

Faith has been very important to my journey. My faith has been a cornerstone. It has been fundamental to my growth. It has been the focal point of my journey. Without faith, I would not have been able to achieve what I have achieved so far. But what is faith?

Faith is not a mere mental assent. It is not just an intellectual agreement with a fact. Faith is a practical demonstration of one's confidence in what God has said, or in the vision that God has given someone. My faith is only demonstrated in the actions that I take in response to what God has told me.

And without faith it is impossible to please God... [Hebrews 11:6 NIV].

Sometimes, a certain experience can inspire your faith. Remember that I first heard about Australia while watching a documentary on BBC about Australia's need for doctors. Interviews showed different international doctors discussing

Navigating Change (My Story)

how Australia had been treating them well. The country was welcoming and the pathway to citizenship was straightforward. I was at a low moment in my life at that time. My dad was sick and things were not going well. I saw that documentary on a Sunday afternoon. On Monday morning, I walked into the hospital (where I was employed as an intern) and saw a poster on the wall with a picture of Professor John Hamilton, the Dean of Medicine from the University of Newcastle, Australia. What a coincidence! He was giving a public lecture on campus ground. I made up my mind to attend. Interestingly, my direct supervisor also happened to be the buddy of Professor Hamilton. She asked me to gather a few of my colleagues to meet with him. This appeared to be like an answer to my prayers for direction.

After my colleagues and I were interviewed by Professor Hamilton, we took a group photo and everybody left. As I was leaving the room, I felt a prompting in my spirit that this was the chance. Faith is not just believing what God has said. I knew that throughout those 24 hours, God had been telling me about Australia. I never even imagined about Australia until I watched the documentary the night before. I turned back to the professor and said, *'Professor, just a quick one. I'd like to come to Australia one day'*. He was surprised. After handing me his business card, he asked me to reach out to him whenever I came. I kept the card in my wallet but did not email him until a year later. He replied to my email a few weeks before my visitor's visa expired and he became my lifeline to getting my first professional job.

Faith is not just agreeing mentally that God loves you and has a certain plan for you, or He wants you to do something. Like Michael Todd, lead pastor of Transformation Church said, *'If you have faith in it, you will put your weight on it'*. If you have faith in God's Word, you will put your weight on it. When we have faith in God's vision for us, we practically manifest it by putting our confidence in it and practicalising it.

Taking the step that day to approach Professor Hamilton boldly and declare to him that I planned to go to Australia was a step of faith, one that God was going to honour. I did not have the resources, but God raised help for me and opened the way in response to the action that I took.

Faith is not just believing that God can. It is believing and trusting that God *will*. If you believe that God will provide, you will make the move, stand, and be able to achieve success. Faith does not exist without trust. Michael Todd said, '*If you can work it out yourself, it is not faith*'. You have to hope and trust in Him; He has gone ahead of you and has made that declaration. God was leading me to Australia. He had gone ahead of me and told me that He wanted me to be in Australia, something I could not do myself. When I looked at how incapable I was, I had doubts and concerns. I quickly learnt that doubts and worries will not take you anywhere. They keep your heart racing and your mind preoccupied but will take you nowhere.

That was exactly how I felt. My thoughts were racing and I was worried and doubtful. Through reflection, I soon realised that obeying God, taking simple steps, and putting my weight on what God had said worked.

The first thing I did was online research – and the more I researched, the more clarity I had about the vision. The first time I called the Australian Medical Council, I spent almost all of my money because I did not realise the calls were so expensive. Every time I called, I would be on hold for almost 45 minutes, which still consumed money. I had to fill in many papers and apply for certification from the United States to make sure my degree was well certified. The further I went through the

Navigating Change (My Story)

process, the clearer the vision became. When we learn to trust God and take simple steps, He responds. Those 'big' things become small. It's just a matter of taking the first, simple step. Once I launched forth, it became easier.

I also shared the vision with my colleagues and we contributed money to buy textbooks. When the books arrived, we photocopied them and shared them amongst ourselves to read because we couldn't afford an original copy each. Out of the five that I shared the vision with, only two are currently practising in Australia. The more I researched, explored, applied myself, and prayed, the clearer the vision became. The initial doubts I had started to go away. With each passing day, I became more confident and stronger. I knew that God was on my side.

Some people said it was not possible. I met a man in the doctor's lounge in Lagos who told me he had just returned from Australia. He sat and passed the exam and spent 12 months in Australia before his visa expired and he had to return. For him, it was a failed project. This was just a few months before I was about to take that step. I asked myself, '*Will I listen to the man who has been there and back, or will I listen to Him who said I should take the bold step to go*'?

I continued studying and did not allow the man's experience to affect me. Throughout this time, my father was sick, so I would study after visiting him. When I ignored the doubts and naysayers and took bold steps, I realised that God showed himself and gave me signs to encourage me.

When I wanted to apply for the tourist visa, people shared their experiences with me. Some people said when they applied, they were granted a visa lasting a few weeks. Another person said he only got a one-week visa to attempt the exam. Almost all these visas had a 'no further stay' condition, meaning you would have to leave the country at all costs once your visa expires. The visa could not be renewed, even if you had a job offer. I clearly did not want that. I could not afford to return to Nigeria.

So, I applied for a three-month tourist visa. One day, I received a phone call from the case officer who was processing my application, which had never happened to me before. By that time, I had already travelled to South Africa and the UK on student exchange and clinical observership programmes. The case officer asked me to provide the phone number of one of my supervisors who could confirm I was employed as a doctor. After giving the phone number to her, I boldly requested that I would prefer NOT to have a 'no-further-stay' condition. Luckily, my visa was approved without this condition. At that time, I did not know anybody else who had been granted a three-month visa without a 'no-further-stay' condition. That opened doors for me.

Trusting God is doing something in response to what God has said. Faith never exists in isolation, otherwise it would just be an intellectual concept that has no meaning. Faith is only meaningful when it is doing something. Faith is never idle, it never sits still; it is always seen in our actions and ideas. It is seen in what we do with our hands, where we go with our legs, and in what we say with our mouths. Faith always does something. It is never faith if it does nothing. It is never faith if it is only thinking. It is never faith if it is only imagining without doing. When it does, and what is done agrees with what has been said and revealed, that is faith.

Navigating Change (My Story)

Challenges to Faith
1. **Fear**

As a neurologist, I inject Botox, a neurotoxin, which paralyses nerves. If you inject too much, you can weaken a muscle. Fear is also a paralytic agent. Fear is the Botox for faith. Fear reduces a man to nothing. In Scripture, after calling down fire on several prophets of Baal and killing all of them, Elijah became afraid, particularly after hearing the terrifying voice of Jezebel. He ran away and escaped. Fear reduced him to a piece of meat.

Fear drains away all the energy from someone, but the good thing is that men of faith who do great things for God are not men *without fear*. They are men who can stand strong despite their fear and fight it. That's what my story has been. There have been many times when I have been enveloped by fear. There were many times I felt I could not do it. There have been many times where I felt that the weight of expectation was so much that I could not deliver, but I realised that every time I looked away from myself and the difficulties and I looked to God, the fear disappeared. He gives me another sign, he gives me hope and strength. He renews me.

Fear will never go away from the heart of man. Dr. Samuel Ekundayo said, 'A God-given dream is usually bigger than you'. In fact, there is no way that God will give you a dream that is bigger than you and you will not have any fear. The weight of expectation will scare you because it is more than your current capacity. As human beings, when we are faced with situations that are beyond us, it is natural for us to cringe, doubt ourselves, and be afraid. The only way we can come out of that is to go back and look up at the one who has called us and given us that vision because He will give us a sign. He will never leave us in the dark. In my darkest moments, when I felt all hope was lost,

He would give me a sign and a word. He would renew my strength and vigour and open up a door.

The other way to overcome fear is to take a step. I took steps with my job, relationships, parents, and family. I have made a lot of mistakes, but every time I have overcome fear, it was not by sitting down and doing nothing. I overcome fear by looking up to God and responding to His call by taking an action. Many times, I am uncertain about the outcome, but I know if I take that step, He will step in. If I don't take that step, there is no way God will step in. God will only respond when we take that step.

A very good example of this in Scripture is when Peter looked out of the boat and saw Jesus from afar, walking on water. Peter called out to Jesus and Jesus told him to come. Peter stepped out of the boat and began to walk on water. As soon as he saw the waves of the sea, he took his eyes off Jesus and began to sink. Thank God Jesus caught his hand. When we look at the waves, the terrifying situations, and obstacles, we will sink. The only thing that will keep us afloat is looking at the Master. That is faith. Without looking, there is no faith. It is only a matter of what you are looking at. Let me explain. A young girl was in a ship that was about to capsize. She was playing in her cabin with her toys when a cabin hostess came to grab her hand and tried to explain why they had to leave. However, the girl felt comfortable and did not want to be bothered. She replied, '*I have nothing to fear because my dad is the captain of this ship*'. Even though there was a lot of commotion, the girl was so confident in her father who had told her to stay in the cabin and play with her toys. She just believed in her heart that there was nothing to worry about. Shortly after, the storm calmed and her father returned for her.

Navigating Change (My Story)

When we look at the mountain, we will be afraid. When we have trust in God, look up to Him, and hold onto His word, we will overcome fear.

2. **Failure**

Failure is a universal denominator that every successful person will have to taste. Failure is important in our growth process and life of faith. I have faced failure in many areas, but one key memory I have is from the first year of my doctoral studies. I had done a clinical study involving over 250 participants, from which I wrote a 'heavily loaded' paper that I thought was ground-breaking. At that time, I had never failed any exam in my life. I had become a specialist physician, so I had a lot of confidence in writing this paper. It was well-referenced and I had a lot of powerful, well-published co-authors. I got the shock of my life when the medical journal I submitted it to rejected the paper. They not only rejected the paper for revision, but they felt that it was not good enough to be published in a local Australian journal! Not even an international journal. That broke my heart because I had put in months of effort and time into it. That was the first time I was rejected in academia. That was the first time I had done something related to my learning and failed. My supervisor said, '*Welcome to being rejected*'.

I was determined not to give up on that paper, so I went back to study. I did more research and recruited more patients, improving the sample size. I did more literature reviews to ensure the paper was properly written. I resubmitted the paper and it was accepted this time. Less than 18 months later, that same paper led to ground-breaking, novel research which won me the Golseth Award, an award for neuromuscular physicians that is granted by the American Association of Neuromuscular & Electrodiagnostic Medicine (AANEM). I was the third

Australian to ever win that award. It seemed a long way from rejection to triumph.

Picture: Winning the Golseth Young Investigator Award of the AANEM in Phoenix Arizona, USA, 2017.

Failure prepares us and tunes us for our destiny. Failure sharpens us and helps us to turn to God. A lot of people walk away from their destiny too early because they feel that when they fail, they have reached the end of the road. The truth is that when we fail, we need to act again in faith and respond to failure with faith by doing. Then, we can overcome.

Navigating Change (My Story)

3. **Family and friends**

Sometimes, when God gives a man or woman a vision, his family and friends may pose big obstacles because they have not seen the vision. God does not usually work with committees; He looks for an individual. When God gives a man or woman a big dream, their immediate family and friends may not see the same thing, so they may judge the vision differently. The first time I conceived the thought that God wanted me to marry my wife, Olayemi, I knew she was the perfect mate for me, but some of my family and friends did not see it that way. They felt I was making a mistake. They may have good reasons for thinking she was not good enough, but I knew exactly what God had shown me. Family and friends may try to put doubt in your heart and say things to minimise the vision, but remember that when God gives us a dream, He can bring it to pass. Sometimes, the opinion of our family and friends may create obstacles for us that may limit the exploits of our faith.

Often, our families come from a good place because they want the best for us, but sometimes they want their own best and not God's best. That's why, when I hear from God or receive a vision or a dream, I try to communicate it to them effectively. If they do not agree, then I can prayerfully wait on God for direction and still take the bold step. At the end of the day, what matters is whether I have fulfilled God's mandate for my life. That's what counts.

The Bible describes when Samuel was going to anoint a king. When he got to David's house, David's father, Jesse, did not parade him as an option when asked to bring out all his sons. David was a teenager at the time, who was in the wilderness looking after his father's sheep. He was not counted because his father did not see him in that role. There are many times our families and friends do not see us living the dreams and visions that God has given us. That's why we must be careful because sometimes our families and friends can be dream killers.

4. **Finances**

When God gives a person a vision, He is obliged to finance it. There are many times that God will lead a person in a direction, but because of the seeming lack of resources, doubt and fear creep in – then they begin to look for alternatives. Many people have left the centre of God's will because of inconvenience. That first job I was offered in Morawa, Western Australia was a very good one, with a six-figure pay, but I knew that contract was meant to keep me there against God's will. The contract came with a lot of bonuses and benefits – free rent, official vehicle, etc. – but based on the visions of my future that God had shown me, I knew that was not what He wanted for me. So, I had to sacrifice the contract for a lower-paying job that would help me to fulfil my dreams. I left a 5-bedroom home to share a 2-bedroom unit with a friend. I went from paying zero bills to paying every single bill, but I had to do that because I knew exactly where I was going. I knew the short-term pain would lead to long-term gain.

One of the things that can hinder faith is the lack of financial power. Many people have walked away from their destinies because of a lack of resources or alternatives.

God asked Abraham to leave his father's house to go to a land He would show him, which was Canaan. When Abraham got to Canaan, the land that God promised to him and his descendants, he built an altar there and he worshipped God, but there was a famine in the land. There are times we will find ourselves in God's will, yet there will be famine. Abraham left his father's house, his wealth, his abundance, and he took a journey to a strange land where there was famine. Unfortunately, Abraham left the land and went to Egypt because of the resources in Egypt. While he was in Egypt, he became rich in cattle and servants. One of those servants was a 13-year-old girl named Hagar, who later became a thorn in his flesh. When he returned to Canaan after some years, he was thankfully still able to fulfil the promise. Many people have travelled to Egypt and were not able to return to fulfil the promise.

Isaac, Abraham's son, faced the same challenge. Genesis chapter 26 described a famine in the land, but the angel of the Lord instructed Isaac not to go into Egypt as his father did. Isaac listened, sowed in the land, and reaped a 100-fold harvest in the same year, in the same land where there was a famine.

This came about because God knows how to finance His vision and our destiny. But, when we leave because of difficulty or make convenient choices, we walk away from God's supernatural provision.

5. **Facts and Fiction**

Whilst fiction is something that is invented: untrue or unproven, facts are true and proven, so we tend to believe them more. Facts and stats sometimes get in the way of the fulfillment of our purpose and our faith. However, the fact that something has not been done before does not mean that it cannot be done. Sometimes, facts – or what we think is true – kills innovation and creativity. That's why some creative companies do not do opinion polls and do not seek validation from people. Facts sometimes limit our creative ability to produce things that have not existed before. There is a saying, *'The man who says it cannot be done is generally interrupted by someone doing it'*.

Many facts exist that will 'prove' to you that you cannot do what you want to do. This weight of evidence may try to convince you that you cannot succeed in what you want to do. In my own life, I have faced those odds. There were many times I looked at the number of people who were working in a particular environment and I realised that the odds were stacked against me. I am just one of two black neurologists in the whole country. When I decided to be a neurologist, I knew that I was going to be working in a white-person-dominated industry in the country. Even though the facts were against me in the selection process, I still applied, and I came through. So, while facts may be true, they may get in the way of faith.

Fiction can also limit us. There are many times we hear fictional stories, but we believe them. Those kinds of myths become truths that people hold onto and spread around. Many people told me that as I was an inexperienced, black intern I would not get a job in a teaching hospital. It was unproven, but I heard it said as fact from different people. A lot of people hold different myths that limit their horizon; stories that make them feel they cannot do it because nobody else has done it. That's fiction. It's unproven and untrue. Sometimes, because we cannot see examples of other people doing what God is calling us to do, we grow weary in our faith and walk away from our purpose or dreams.

Lesson: It is important to be careful of myths and truths, as both can limit our minds.

Chapter 7

Persistence

It was six years ago. This girl needed to talk to someone. Someone she could share her heart-felt reflections and her deepest worries with. She thought I had answers to her many puzzles, or at least I could give intelligent suggestions.

Her eyes sparkled with excitement at my very sight and she gave me a warm welcome. She seemed glad I had kept the date. But like in an illusion, she had meticulously drafted a fictitious sketch of me in her mind. She had pictured me as a happy and auspicious young man, endowed with the sweetest gratifications life had to offer.

Things were not as they used to be for her. The joy she had enjoyed all her life was fast ebbing away, like a wisp of smoke, and her burdened heart cried out for succour. Simply put, she was not happy.

My easygoing 'how are you?' was enough to unlock the floodgates of her heavy heart. That simple enquiry led to a massive spate of tales.

She poured out her heart like a train's steam engine – scene after scene, episode after episode. It was like watching one of Jack Bauer's stunts in 24, leaving you with suspense and great emotion. I was engulfed by the gravity of her experiences, looking through her eyes; I could see the pain of her heart. She needed a word – a word loaded with grace, charged with faith, full of inspiration, and declared with conviction.

Wondering what word could calm her turbulent soul, I felt led to do a strange thing. In a daring move, I began to share with her my own ordeal and so I subtly distracted her from her worries. Although I had put up a cheerful facade, my world was crumbling fast too – I wasn't a happy man either. At least we had something else in common, apart from being mates.

That discovery of my vulnerability was embarrassing to her. It burst her bubble and dashed into pieces the delicate mental portrait she had of me. Soon she realised I was not the 'big boy' she assumed I was. And it worked in a dramatic fashion. There was an abrupt switch in her mental attitude; she changed her posture to her problems. Rather than sulk and whine, she became positive and thankful. She was not alone in her present ordeal. Hers was not the worst of trials – mine neither – and she realised she had to bear her cross with a smile. That made a lot of difference.

Weeks later, I got an anonymous package, which contained a brown envelope and many other things that a hustling campus boy would need. In the envelope was an anonymous letter. *'Could this have been from her? Maybe the fellowship's welfare unit has remembered God's humble servant'*, I thought. Coded

Navigating Change (My Story)

in that letter was one of the most inspiring messages I have ever received. It gladdened my heart and lit up the candle of my soul. It was a handwritten masterpiece, simple in construct, but full of life. Few people have touched me that deeply — she touched my very core!

The letter ended with these gracious words: '*You deserve to be happy*'! When I saw those words, I knew the author. The next day, I asked her, '*Did you send me any package yesterday*'? But she refused to comment. Then I whispered, '*You deserve to be happy*'! Her only response was an affectionate smile.

Yes, I deserve to be happy. Having an understanding of who I am changed my mental attitude and my feelings. I was not going to sulk and look for sympathy. I was not going to settle for an average, middling, or mediocre life. Once I understood my purpose and saw my potential, I was fired up for my pursuit of excellence.

Persistence is only possible when you understand your purpose and identity. Your identity is who you really are, while your purpose explains *why* you are who you are. When you understand who you are and why you have been designed the way you are, you will stay in your lane and receive the confidence and hope necessary to hang in there and continue with your journey. A lot of people do not persist in their journey in life because they do not foresee their destination.

Persistence is an important attribute for anybody bound for success because it is unnatural to stay on course, especially when there are no immediate results. It is difficult to commit to a process that does not yield instant benefits. Persistence is an intentional and voluntary submission to a course even though there is no immediate gratification. The ability to submit yourself to that process can only be sustained by the revelation or vision of a future and a hope that there will be light at the end of the tunnel. The ability to stay the course and weather the storm is key. Every successful person across all generations, of all races, and different backgrounds, have this common quality – persistence.

I'm a very optimistic person and I have realised that my optimism is born out of the same source as my persistence. My optimism feeds my persistence. My optimism stems from the fact that I have a positive view of the future and I know that my current position does not define me. I know that there is hope for the future. That hope is what keeps me going.

When we were building our house, I had to do an inspection when it was 50 percent completed. The house did not look attractive and I could not imagine where everything would be. However, I had a mental picture of the future house, which is what kept us going through the process (as well as the contract we signed). Throughout my life, I have experienced so many obstacles and challenges in my family, my relationships, and the relocation from Nigeria to Australia, but what has kept me going is my ability to *hang in there* no matter how tough it may be.

Stay the Course
My wife and I had a calling and a leading to start a church around the same time as I started my specialist practice. One of my lowest moments was showing up to church after spending hours preparing a message, and there were only ten people present. My spirit was so down, somewhere near the floor of the church. I wondered how I was going to preach a one-hour message to ten

Navigating Change (My Story)

people, two of whom were my children. Before the message started, I kept looking back and hoping somebody new would show up. God told me, '*Preach to these few as though you were preaching to a thousand*'. I took that word, climbed the pulpit, and preached as though I was preaching to a thousand. I just kept swinging.

One phrase we use in Beautiful Gate Parish where I pastor is, 'keep swinging'. No matter what comes, just keep swinging. Fight one more round – because the man that fights one more round is never knocked out. His face may be bruised and his body may be battered, but he will never be knocked out. He may fall many times, but he will always rise again before the end of the count. And so it is with your life.

Pictures: At Beautiful Gate, Sydney.

The next day, I turned up to work in my new practice with my suit and my briefcase. I had only three patients booked, so I thought it was going to be a quick day. Alas, no one turned up. All the patients cancelled on me, so I had no income for the day. On Sunday, I had a congregation of fewer than ten people and on Monday, I had no patients. I felt so bad that week and I was filled with doubts. The church was just about a month old, while my practice was around two months old then. But I had learnt about persistence. I dreamt about the church becoming more robust, having our venue, and owning our property, which kept me going. Every Sunday, I would turn up and preach as if I was preaching to 1000 people, which I knew I would do one day. I had clearly heard God say that, so I turned up every Sunday and did what I had to do, deliberately and with intention because I knew the vision would come to pass.

Similarly, with my business, it has swung the other way. I am now booked out three months in advance in all three of my practices. As I write this, I will be working during my days off

Navigating Change (My Story)

this week because my waiting list is so long. I have had to create extra sessions for patients on the waiting list to see me.

That is the power of persistence. When you stay true to your calling, believe in your dreams, and keep swinging even though the tides are against you, you will breakthrough. The success will come.

Zig Ziglar said, *'Success is not a destination, it is a journey'*. For me, true success is not in the outcome, but in the process that produces the outcome. What makes me successful is not what I have now, but who I have become after going through the challenges I have experienced. For me, the process that delivers the outcome or miracle is much more important than the miracle itself.

When I was doing my Ph.D., I had to wake up at 5 a.m. every morning to beat the traffic on the way to the hospital in the city. I was recruiting and studying patients with kidney disease who were on dialysis to learn about how dialysis affects nerve function. This period was difficult because I had a young family. My wife worked permanent night shifts on Sundays, so she had to take our son to work with her. He had to sleep in the nurses' common room while she was at work because I had to leave the house very early in the morning. I realised that doing this every day built resilience in me, and I got to know my craft better. Even though it was difficult to persist with, I was proud of my work when I was called onto the stage to receive my doctorate, knowing I had done a novel study. I received the dean's award for the most outstanding thesis in the school. It was tough, but the process was much more important than the outcome. For me, the skills I learnt during the doctorate were more important than the three letters after my name.

I am reminded of the story of a wolf pack. They can hunt out the trail of a herd of prey from kilometres away before finding them. Even though they cannot see them, they follow the trail, sometimes for days. They persist through rough terrain, pain, and difficulty. They may not be able to see the prey, but they can perceive them. I imagine that the mother wolf who leads the pack may often be questioned by the younger wolves, but she'd encourage them to keep moving, even though they cannot see the prey yet.

If you can perceive a ray of light, keep swinging. Very soon, a breakthrough will occur. Eventually, the wolf pack will be right in the midst of their prey. This long path teaches the wolf pack patience. Through this, they develop resistance and resilience in order to wear out their prey. They must trust their instincts, follow the process, and work as a team.

DETOURS

The journey of life cannot always be straight and smooth. There are always hills, rough spots, and occasional detours. A detour is a long way around the main route to your destination. It often takes you off the best path but brings you back to the main road after much inconvenience. The word 'detour' is from a French root word, meaning a change of direction. There are many times we experience detours on the pathway to our destiny, but one of the biggest keys to sustaining our dream is to recognise the gold in our detours. There is a temptation for us to think that our detour is a distraction and we need to move back to the main road, but that may be wrong. God often allows us to go through detours before he takes us to our destiny. He allows this so He can prepare our destination for us and also prepare us for our destination. And so, he takes us through detours to develop us

Navigating Change (My Story)

for the destiny He has for us. All in all, detours are very important.

When I finished high school, I wrote and passed my matriculation exams. I thought I had done enough to be accepted into the university, but that did not happen. I had also written another entrance exam for a college. I got an excellent result – I was the third-best student in the whole country. Soon after, I received a letter in the mail offering me a place in the college to study computer science for a diploma. That was not my first choice. It wasn't what I wanted, but since I could not get into medical school, I took on the challenge and went to study computer science. I learnt computer programming and how to develop different applications. I applied myself, even though I had to study mathematics and calculus, things that I was naturally gifted for, but was not keen on. I always wanted to be a physician because I thought I could help and interact with people. Moreover, I believed I had the gift of interacting with, talking to, and helping vulnerable people, but computer science was a different world to me. All I had to do was sit behind a machine and type, hoping that my programme did not have bugs. Yet, I applied myself. I did not know exactly what I was doing there, but I tried my best.

Looking back, that was one of the best periods of my life, though I did not recognise it at the time. I had no money or anything. The church that I attended was paying my fees throughout the degree. I usually went to school by faith, without any money for lunch or transport fare back home, but I learnt to trust God every single day. My neighbour usually helped me with transport fare. Somehow, lunch would be provided during the day, and somehow, I always made it back home safely. That was when I really learnt what it means to trust God.

In my last year in college, I took the entrance exam again for medical school. I made a covenant with God that if I got into medical school, I would serve Him for the rest of my life. When I passed the exam, I quickly ran to the church and thanked God for making my dream come true. At the time, we had no money, no food, my mother had no job to take care of the five kids (my dad had already left home then), yet there I was, getting into medical school. I had no idea how, but I just knew it was going to happen. God was going to make it happen for me.

After that, I had to complete my final year project in college, so I decided to design an automated medical billing system for a private hospital as a way to sign out of the Computer Science degree. I got an excellent score on the project and received a distinction grade (the equivalent of a first-class grade) in my final semester in college. Even though it was not my purpose, I applied myself.

Applying myself also led to getting a distinction in calculus. I knew I was good at it, but it wasn't what I wanted. However, I learnt to trust God every single day. By the time I got to medical school, that detour was worth it for me. I had just given my life to Christ when I started college, so that detour was when God really built me up. I met wonderful people, some of whom are still my friends today. I built great networks and God strengthened and solidified me.

God took me through that detour to develop me for my destiny. During that time, I learnt to trust Him and decided to serve Him forever. If I had gone straight to medical school, I do not know what may have happened to my relationship with Christ. Additionally, through that detour, God was preparing my destination for when I arrived by ensuring that everything that I needed was ready. At the time I received the offer of a place at

Navigating Change (My Story)

college, nothing was ready for me to successfully function in medical school, so that detour needed to happen for everything to come together for the destination to be worthwhile.

Detours are often unexpected. They come up suddenly, appearing without notice. If God decided to warn us about all the detours we are going to go through, we would never submit ourselves to the process. If Joseph in the Bible knew all the detours he would have to go through for him to be prepared for destiny and vice versa, he would never have gone through it.

As well as being unpredictable in their timing, detours are often slow. Have you ever driven down the main road that is under construction only to see a detour sign? You'd have to go around the block, usually with a lower speed limit and with a lot of turns, bends, and sometimes traffic. It is often slow and teaches us patience and reliance on God. If it is an area that you are not familiar with, you will have to depend on GPS and road signs because it is unpredictable.

An individual needs to be able to recognise God's work in their detours so that they will not think a detour is a distraction and a waste of time. Just the way I saw that God was building me up for the future through my detours in life, you can see God in your detours as well.

If you do not see God in your detour, you will not learn the lesson that He wants you to learn through that experience. If all you see is pain, discomfort, and delay, you will not learn and appreciate the lesson. If you stick to the same route you are familiar with or the same route your predecessors have travelled, you will make a shipwreck of your journey, but if you stick with God as he leads you through the detour, He will bring you out the other side.

When you make it out from the other side, you would have bypassed all the dangers along the main way. You will be ready for your destiny, and your destiny will be ready for you.

Lesson: Detours are often uneven, rough, and winding. They often point us to God so that we can depend and lean on him. These key characteristics of detours help us grow.

Picture: Donating a Nerve Conduction Study machine to the Lagos State University Teaching Hospital in Nigeria

Navigating Change (My Story)

Picture: Giving back. Donation of medical equipment to my medical school in Nigeria

Picture: Training doctors in Nigeria

Epilogue

My life has not been a bed of roses. I have experienced many different challenges in life, and I have also enjoyed some success. I have learned to accept the pain of the loss of a father. I have also experienced the joy of being a father and watching my babies' first cry. I have watched my mum cry tears of pain from being hurt by her loved one. I have also seen the joy pour out of my wife from the affection of a loved one. I know what it means to be rejected, despite trying to please everyone. I also know what it means to be accepted by everyone. I know what it means to wake up in the morning, having nothing to eat. I also know what it means to go to bed with a full stomach. I know what it means to not have a dime for transport fare, but I also know what it means to go on a holiday via a first-class cabin.

In short, I have learnt to prosper. I have learnt to thrive, even when I have nothing. And I have learnt to have hope and joy when I had something.

I cannot say I have experienced it all, but I think I can say that I have experienced some of life. I know my trials are not the worst of trials, and my successes are not the most outstanding. However, I know that if you've read the book this far, then my story would have resonated with you. My story may not be unique, but I am unique. That makes my message unique. My message is one of navigating change during a time of crisis. No matter the hand you are played, no matter what side of the coin is flipped towards you, you must resolve to apply the principles in this book to make a difference.

Navigating Change (My Story)

Niyi Borire

Pictures: At our traditional Nigerian wedding – 9 years after we got married.

Conclusion

Remember that you get more from life when you have a positive approach to every situation you find yourself. Furthermore, it is impossible to navigate change if you have not yet discovered your purpose. You can only be at your best when you are at your purpose. You can only survive change when you are in your purpose.

Never forget that you will need to lean on people close to you to survive change. Relationships are the pillars of growth in times of change. Fostering healthy relationships will keep you grounded and accountable, as well as help you to maintain your identity and individuality in a time of change.

You will also need to be a person of integrity and persistence if you are going to be able to blaze the trail and come out on top. Integrity gives you a legitimate claim to victory.

You must never allow anything to reduce the height and breadth of your dreams. You must have the fortitude to believe in the beauty of your dreams, even when they seem impossible.

Finally, faith creates an atmosphere for possibilities. Faith sustains our expectations in a time of change. As you have seen in my journey, my faith in God is reflected in my walk with Him. I would like you to have a similar experience. All you need to do is believe in your heart and accept the gift of salvation that God has made available for you. If you have not received Jesus Christ into your life as your Lord and Saviour, you can do it right now. Just pray this simple prayer:

'Dear God, I acknowledge that my life is not complete without you. I appreciate your gift of salvation through the sacrifice of your son and I wholeheartedly accept this gift of salvation. I

receive Jesus as my Lord and personal saviour in Jesus's name. Amen. Thank you, Jesus. I am a child of God'.

If you have prayed this prayer, I am glad you did. Please let me know about your experience and about how this book has impacted your life. You can reach me at info@niyiborire.com

Your Key to Navigating Change

Navigating change starts by being intentional about your growth. You cannot afford to settle for an average, middling, mediocre life. That's why I found this anthology worth sharing with the world. The little things we do matter. Tiny droplets of water mount up to produce an overflow. This implies that if you practise the principles extracted from the lessons I have shared, you would be mapping your journey to greatness.

This journey will at times be tough, and tough times demand tough sacrifices. No great person became great through dreaming alone. They put in the work. Through this journey, you will evolve and grow to become an extraordinary person. Now is the time to follow these principles. Now is the time to navigate change successfully.

Navigating change will require the very most you can give and the best qualities you can develop. Be reminded that when opportunities don't come, you must create them. This was what I did when I had no job opportunity in Australia. I went back to my drawing board and created an opportunity for myself. This led to my breakthrough. Think outside the box, always.

Growth during a time of change is optional. It has to be deliberately pursued and it would require taking the time to apply all the knowledge you have acquired from this book, even

Navigating Change (My Story)

in the face of challenges and potential failure on the way. If you have read this book to this point, you probably have big aspirations already. This book may motivate you to pursue your dreams, but remember motivation would keep you going, but discipline will keep you growing. Never allow procrastination, fear, or laziness to deprive you of your growth.

This is your time. This is your moment. Make it count. Stop waiting for the big break. Go for your goals and pursue your dreams. I look forward to hearing your testimonies of success, as you navigate change.

Dr. Niyi Borire, MBBS FRACP Ph.D.

Transformational Speaker & Change Agent info@niyiborire.com

Director, Southwest Neurology southwestneurology.com.au

Consultant Neurologist and Clinical Neurophysiologist

Liverpool Hospital, St George & Sydney Southwest Private Hospitals

Conjoint Lecturer, Prince of Wales Clinical School, UNSW Australia

Presiding Minister, Beautiful Gate Sydney beautifulgate.com.au

Navigating Change (My Story)

Commentary

Sharing my thoughts on greatness is a dream come true. Having my acquaintances share theirs is even more special to me. This section is dedicated to quoting what four people have to say about me, their lessons from their association with me, and their lessons from life. I hope you pick up a thing or two from them.

Picture: *My family*

Adeniyi Borire is my husband. I have known him for over 15 years now. I have personally learnt a lot from him. If we have to live a life at all, it has to be a life that has God at the centre of it. For him, the pursuit of God is the most important thing in his life.

I have learnt how to be a go-getter from him. He is a go-getter himself. He is someone that pursues his dreams even when there are challenges and difficult situations. He does not give up. He does everything possible to make sure those dreams come to reality. He only gives up if God is saying he should not pursue the dream. But if God gives him the go-ahead, he would do everything possible to make sure the dreams come true. Adeniyi doesn't accept defeat too quickly. When he wants something, he wants it.

The highlights for me are: Never write off anyone when God has not written them off. Never give up on yourself. Sometimes, we go through tough times and think that is the end for us. But it's important to keep pursuing your dreams and following hard after it, and someday, you will reap the fruits of pursuing these things. If God is taken out of our lives and the equation, we become nothing. It is important to pursue God.

My dear wife: **Olayemi Borire**

Registered Nurse

Navigating Change (My Story)

Adeniyi is my very good friend. In fact, he is more than a brother. I have known him for over 20 years. He was my roommate back in school and we did virtually everything together – preaching, eating, playing, etc.

I have learnt a lot from his life. He is a hard worker and fighter. He has a 'never say no' spirit. He is a risk-taker. Those are some of the things about him that are very inspiring. He loves God and God loves him. He has taken many steps in life that sometimes when we discuss, we wonder how it turned out. It always turned out well.

True success in life answers to the combination of talents and efforts. Adeniyi is gifted intellectually. But does he go to sleep and let his results become a product of talents alone? No! He works hard as if his success depends only on his efforts. He combines hard work and efforts with his talents. He was always top of the class in school as he studied hard.

He is a giver. He is compassionate and easily touched by the infirmity and suffering of others. He can give his last kobo or even his school fees just to help someone. He lives a broken life. He is eager to talk about his weaknesses to you as he is willing to talk about his strengths. He is loveable and accountable to people. These for me, stand out.

My good friend: **Doctor Alabi Folorunsho**

MD, Cardinal Academy of Emergency Care

Adeniyi is a bosom friend of mine. I have known him for 7 years. His life is an inspiration and I have learnt lessons from him. I believe life is governed by laid down principles and when these principles are followed to the letter, they will lead to success, regardless of who applies them and their location. I will call the principles the 4 Ds; desire (a strong force that drives an individual vision or dream until it is materialised), determination (firmness of purpose), discipline (self-control), and diligence (working hard to become skilled at what you do). It is worthy of note that my good friend, Adeniyi Borire, possesses these four attributes.

My good friend: **John Adeyemi**

Practising Tele-Communications Engineer.

Australian Registered Migration Agent.

Zonal Pastor, The Redeemed Christian Church of God, Sydney, Australia.

Navigating Change (My Story)

I have known Pastor Adeniyi Borire for over a decade now. During this time, I have known him to be a true child of God, a man who loves his family, a destiny helper, and someone who always pursues opportunities to make his environment and those around him better.

One of the many lessons life has taught me is that you only have a brief moment on the surface of the earth and you must make hay while the sun shines. This is what Pastor Niyi has done by writing his life's story into this short book.

Olabisi Adeyinka,
Pastor, RCCG Australia Region, Province 2.

MY GIFT TO YOU

Thanks for purchasing and reading this book. I have no doubt that you have been blessed and inspired by reading it. Please go to the link below to download my gift to you. I wrote the book, **The Diary of a Brainiac**, to express my purpose and values in my chosen profession as a neurologist, how my career syncs with my ultimate purpose of being a pioneer of change, and how my profession aids my mission as a people-builder.

www.niyiborire.com/books

www.ingramcontent.com/pod-product-compliance
Lightning Source LLC
Chambersburg PA
CBHW021410290426
44108CB00010B/465